HBR Guide to
Designing Your Retirement

Harvard Business Review Guides

Arm yourself with the advice you need to succeed on the job, from the most trusted brand in business. Packed with how-to essentials from leading experts, the HBR Guides provide smart answers to your most pressing work challenges.

The titles include:

HBR Guide for Women at Work

HBR Guide to AI Basics for Managers

HBR Guide to Being a Great Boss

HBR Guide to Being More Productive

HBR Guide to Better Business Writing

HBR Guide to Better Mental Health at Work

HBR Guide to Building Your Business Case

HBR Guide to Buying a Small Business

HBR Guide to Changing Your Career

HBR Guide to Coaching Employees

HBR Guide to Collaborative Teams

HBR Guide to Critical Thinking

HBR Guide to Data Analytics Basics for Managers

HBR Guide to Dealing with Conflict

HBR Guide to Delivering Effective Feedback

HBR Guide to Designing Your Retirement

HBR Guide to Emotional Intelligence

HBR Guide to Executing Your Strategy

HBR Guide to Finance Basics for Managers

HBR Guide to Getting the Mentoring You Need

HBR Guide to Getting the Right Job

HBR Guide to Getting the Right Work Done

HBR Guide to Leading Teams

HBR Guide to Making Better Decisions

HBR Guide to Making Every Meeting Matter

HBR Guide to Managing Flexible Work

HBR Guide to Managing Strategic Initiatives

HBR Guide to Managing Stress at Work

HBR Guide to Managing Up and Across

HBR Guide to Motivating People

HBR Guide to Navigating the Toxic Workplace

HBR Guide to Negotiating

HBR Guide to Networking

HBR Guide to Office Politics

HBR Guide to Performance Management

HBR Guide to Persuasive Presentations

HBR Guide to Project Management

HBR Guide to Remote Work

HBR Guide to Setting Your Strategy

HBR Guide to Smarter Networking

HBR Guide to Thinking Strategically

HBR Guide to Unlocking Creativity

HBR Guide to Work-Life Balance

HBR Guide to Your Job Search

HBR Guide to Your Professional Growth

HBR Guide to
Designing Your Retirement

HARVARD BUSINESS REVIEW PRESS

Boston, Massachusetts

Library of Congress Cataloging-in-Publication Data

Names: Harvard Business Review Press, issuing body.
Title: HBR guide to designing your retirement.
Other titles: Harvard Business Review guide to designing your retirement. | Harvard business review guides.
Description: Boston, Massachusetts : Harvard Business Review Press, [2023] | Series: HBR guides | Includes index.
Identifiers: LCCN 2022057881 (print) | LCCN 2022057882 (ebook) | ISBN | 9781647824914 (paperback) | ISBN 9781647824921 (epub)
Subjects: LCSH: Retirement—Planning. | Retirement—Psychological aspects. | Decision making.
Classification: LCC HQ1062 .H278 2023 (print) | LCC HQ1062 (ebook) | DDC 646.7/9—dc23/eng/20230223
LC record available at https://lccn.loc.gov/2022057881
LC ebook record available at https://lccn.loc.gov/2022057882

ISBN: 978-1-64782-491-4
eISBN: 978-1-64782-492-1

What You'll Learn

A clear calendar. A casual wardrobe. Unhurried mornings. Time to pursue your own agenda. When you think of retirement, what comes to mind? Do you romanticize it, daydreaming about how wonderful life will be when you're beholden to no one and most everything you do is elective? Do you catastrophize it, worrying that you won't have enough money or good health or good company to enjoy it? Or somewhere in between? We know there's no universal age for or definition of retirement anymore—but is there *any* standard or structure for us to lean on?

However you define it, retirement is one of life's major transitions, one that you should prepare for and think about deeply long before you send that final "so long, keep in touch" email to colleagues and clients. But throughout our careers many of us are too busy pursuing our professional goals to think about what lies beyond it. And even when we do devote thought to retirement, we often spend so much time thinking about the financial and medical implications of growing older that we don't think about what it will mean to our sense of self. We are drilled early on that "planning for retirement" means saving money and investing it wisely. But no one seems to focus on what planning for retirement means beyond that, save for clichés about track suits, golf, and card games. We know we'll no longer be spending 40+ hours a week working, but how will we fill that time in a way that brings us joy, fills us with a sense of purpose, and allows us to give back? Will we stop work altogether? Will we start up a business we've always dreamed of? Will we begin a new act, as a teacher, volunteer, coach, or mentor?

Whether you're thinking ahead in the early stage of your career, planning to wind down in the next five years, or already retired and feeling adrift, this guide will help you translate your passions, skills, and experience into this new season of life. You'll learn how to:

- Define what retirement means for you

- Identify possibilities and paths beyond traditional retirement

- Build a bridge between your old work identity and your new sense of self

- Consider creating an encore career to gain income, find meaning, and give back

- Move forward from an unexpected early retirement

- Use job crafting to parlay work skills into leisure and civic activities

- Apply your knowledge and experience to board service or consulting

- Discuss your plans and dreams with those closest to you

- Take proactive steps to manage the stress of the transition

- Cultivate new sources of purpose through relationships, service to others, and embracing life's big questions

Contents

Introduction: Retirement Is a Transition
(Not an Ending)   1
Reimagine and redefine retirement for yourself.
BY HERMINIA IBARRA

SECTION ONE

What Is Retirement Now?

1. **Next-Gen Retirement**   11
   *Post-career life has changed, and it
   demands a new approach.*
   BY HEATHER C. VOUGH, CHRISTINE D. BATAILLE,
   LEISA SARGENT, AND MARY DEAN LEE

2. **How Retirement Changes Your
   Identity . . . and Your Life**   21
   And two processes to see you through it.
   AN INTERVIEW WITH TERESA M. AMABILE
   BY CURT NICKISCH

Contents

SECTION TWO

Define Retirement for Yourself

3. **Design a Retirement That Excites You**   41

   Broaden your range of possibilities.

   BY JEFF GIESEA

4. **What Surviving Pandemic Lockdowns
   Can Teach Us About Major Life Changes**   51

   *Lasting change happens when we go
   through a three-part cycle.*

   BY HERMINIA IBARRA

5. **How to Craft a Better Retirement**   59

   Start small and experiment.

   BY ROB BAKER

6. **Retire with Purpose**   71

   Cultivate new sources of meaning.

   BY JOHN COLEMAN

7. **Learn to Get Better at Transitions**   83

   *Retirement is a big transition, yes.
   But you still have more ahead of you.*

   BY AVIVAH WITTENBERG-COX

SECTION THREE

Consider Your Options—and
Ways Forward

8. **Plan a Satisfying Retirement**   93

   *You're still you; you just may apply your old
   skills in a new encore career.*

   BY REBECCA KNIGHT

9. How to Figure Out What You Want to
   Do When You "Grow Up"   101
   *Whether you're 10, 20, 30, or more years
   away from retirement.*

   BY GORICK NG

10. Reeling from a Sudden Job Loss? Here's
    How to Start Healing   111
    When you had no time to plan.

    BY SILVIANA FALCON AND KANDI WIENS

11. How to Become a Coach or Consultant
    After You Retire   119
    *Flexible hours, location independence—
    and a chance to share what you know.*

    BY DORIE CLARK

12. Are You Ready to Serve on a Board?   127
    *Don't let your skills and experience
    go to waste.*

    BY ANTHONY HESKETH, JO SELLWOOD-TAYLOR,
    AND SHARON MULLEN

13. The Leader's Guide to Retirement   137
    *Plan your off-ramp, take your time, and
    give back.*

    BY MARC A. FEIGEN AND RONALD A. WILLIAMS

SECTION FOUR

Make Choices

14. Deciding on a Drastic Change   147
    *Recognize and address bias to make
    better decisions.*

    BY MARK MORTENSEN

Contents

15. Emotions Aren't the Enemy of Good
Decision-Making   157

*Make better decisions by identifying how you
feel now—and how you'd like to feel after
you've faced a major choice.*

BY CHERYL STRAUSS EINHORN

SECTION FIVE

Retirement Is Hard—Don't Go It Alone

16. Build Your Retirement Board of Directors   165

*It takes a team to figure out what your next
steps will be.*

BY PRISCILLA CLAMAN

17. Relationships and Your Retirement   175

*Write the most important people into your
retirement story from the very beginning.*

BY TERESA M. AMABILE

18. Retirement Is Stressful   189

*But you can take steps to put the "gold" in
the golden years.*

BY RUTH C. WHITE

SECTION SIX

Define Success for Yourself

19. How Will You Measure Your Life?   205

It's not too late to live a life you're proud of.

BY CLAYTON M. CHRISTENSEN

Index   *221*

Retirement Is a Transition (Not an Ending)

by Herminia Ibarra

Across the world, people are reinventing what it means to "retire." As we live longer productive lives, the old 65ish goalpost is giving way to a large variety of ways and times for withdrawal from the world of full-time, paid work. And although retirement used to be top of mind only for those of us in our 50s and beyond, more early-career folks are thinking about the end of their working life at the beginning of their career and whether that journey in between is long or short.

Today, people of all ages are asking themselves profound questions about how much work they do (if at all), what work they do, and the place of work—physically and psychologically—in their lives. Yes, early retirement rates are up in parts of the world where we get to choose when we stop working but so is starting the business you've always dreamed of, returning to school to study something new, getting hired back at your old company as a consultant—without the benefits, but getting paid more (and feeling like you're truly valued)—and many other ways of reinventing the later stages of our careers. Rather than retiring to a life of leisure, just as often we're learning new tricks, pursuing old or newfound passions, and building portfolios, brands, or businesses that align more closely with our values and caretaking responsibilities.

Research studies, many cited in the chapters in this volume, support the trends we are seeing in our friends and family. According to a Federal Reserve Board study, a full one-third of those who retire eventually reverse retirement and return to work on either a full- or part-time basis.[1] Even the Department of Labor has noticed the increase in the labor force participation rates by those 65 and older.[2] In 1985, only 10.8% of those over 65 were working. That number has nearly doubled and is growing. In fact, a study by the Gerontological Society of America reports that people 55 and older are the fastest-growing segment of the American workforce.[3] Some of this is due to necessity: Increases in the cost of living coupled with inadequate pensions mean that people in the lowest income groups are most apt to return to work after retirement. But, the percentage of returners, 35%, is also as high in the highest income groups, as more affluent retirees return to some form of professional work after a year or so to rest and renew.[4] For some, retirement is no longer defined as the total cessation of work, but as work in a new direction, or work with fewer hours.

The options for what kind of work we do in the later stages of our careers, once known as retirement, are no longer limited to volunteer roles and creative endeavors: They include a return to full-time employment, gig work (the share of workers who are self-employed rises markedly with age), starting your own business (people age 55+ make up 21% of the U.S. population, but that age group owns a disproportionately high 50.9% of U.S. small businesses, according to survey data from 3,000 entrepreneurs), social entrepreneurship, or a portfolio of some of these options.[5]

Here's the catch: More people are embracing new forms of work beyond traditional retirement age. But that does not make the personal experience of moving to a new stage of life and work any easier. Longevity has heralded the end of a "lockstep," three-stage life, in which a cohort of people of the same age go through a short learning period (university), a long working period, and a variable leisure period (retirement) at more or less the same time.

As Lynda Gratton and Andrew Scott argued in their book *The 100-Year Life*, if we are now living decades longer than when retirement was first invented, it makes no sense to simply further stretch out the long working period between our twenties and sixties; nor does it make sense to retire from a productive life when we are still at the height of our powers. Instead, it becomes logical to transition more frequently between periods of learning, working, and leisure. According to *Forbes*, for example, going back to school after age 50 is the new normal.[6] A great illustration of this sort of jibing and tacking is Kevin who, in his role as captain of a submarine at age 50, wasn't ready for retirement from the navy. So, he enrolled in law school (he already had an engineering degree) and wound up working as a lawyer for the U.S. Department of Veterans Affairs, helping veterans with appeals, ultimately becoming a judge before his second retirement (so far) at age 74.

The new rule is that there are no rules. There are countless possible stages to our lives. We're making it up as we go along, changing the face of retirement as our parents knew it. That's exciting. And also scary.

What This Book Will Do

This book will help you think deeply about your skills and interests to design a retirement that works uniquely for you. It will help you plan, individually or with your life partner. This book will also help you if you're already in the throes of a retirement transition, if you had neither the time nor the bandwidth to plan before stepping out and are now looking for guidance on possible next steps. Whether you are choosing retirement on your own terms or faced with mandatory retirement rules that leave you no choice about the timing of this transition, the ideas covered in this collection will help you think through what you want and how to go about getting it. Although people approaching retirement age may be the most apt to pick up this volume, anyone at any age or career stage, even early-career folks, can be thinking about retirement, not just as an end goal for their career journey but, increasingly, as a vital phase of renewal in today's nonlinear careers.

(And What This Book Will Not Do)

This book will not help you gauge whether you can afford to retire, or how to manage the financial aspects of life when you're no longer receiving a steady stream of income. This book will not help you assess your health and any present or possible conditions that may limit your possibilities. This book will not help you sort through any tangled legal documents as you separate from a partnership or close an LLC or make plans for your estate. Consultation with relevant professional advisers in any of these areas that you may be concerned about is one of the first steps you should take.

Navigate the Transition

Having spent the greater part of my career studying all sorts of transitions in our working life—and as I conduct research for a new book on navigating later career stages—I can point to three observations about retirement, echoed in the chapters in this book: retirement is a transition that challenges your sense of identity, transitions have unavoidable messy middles, and the only way through to a fulfilling next phase is to experiment with new activities, new networks, and new stories about ourselves.

Retirement is a transition, not merely an objective change of role or status but a process of moving from a known past working life to a yet unknown future. The "known" that becomes unclear and uncertain is who you are, your sense of identity. That's because work is so central to how we define ourselves. Work shapes how we spend our time, the company we keep for the bulk of our waking hours, and the story we tell ourselves and others about who we are and how we became that. No matter how much we want and plan for that next chapter, losing those pillars is tough. Section one will help you think through the impact of your retirement on your identity.

Second, **the hallmark of all transition is a messy, middle period**, an interregnum between old and new in which we tend to struggle, caught in a vortex of conflicting desires, confusing options, and a big dollop of uncertainty. This period can start long before a formal end date, and it can extend quite some time after it. But there is no avoiding it. In fact, it is a good thing, a sign that we are actively grappling with the big existential questions. The messy middle is the crucible for a new you. It simply takes longer and greater reflection to design the right retirement than to foreclose on possibilities. No pain, no gain. That's why the most common piece of advice that retiring people get is: Don't make any long-term commitments right away. You need distance from the throes of your old life to figure out what future you really want. Section two will help you define retirement for yourself, and section three will help you identify and evaluate your options.

Third, **the only way through a transition is to experiment and learn**, iterating your way to a bespoke next phase that is right for you. Yes, you can plan ahead, but you simply can't figure it all out in your head. Even people who claim to know exactly what they want to do next (or what they never want to do again) easily find themselves doing something completely different three years later. So, stop trying to set a specific destination before you take the first steps. Try out new roles, projects, and activities, provisionally. Make your way into new networks, find kindred spirits, "guides" who have done it before you, and communities of peers reaching for the same things you care about. Tell your story to anyone who will listen and modify and revise it as you learn more about yourself. These are your tools for re-invention. Sections four, five, and six will help you make choices, find the support you need, and ensure you're living into your values.

If we are lucky enough to be reasonably healthy and reasonably solvent, and to benefit from supportive relationships (admittedly, a tall order), this new life stage can offer extraordinary freedom to reinvent ourselves on our own terms and devote our time to what we truly choose to do. But, so many of us still dread the necessary transition, fail to prepare, and as a result, risk remaining stuck in the presumed safety of the past. This book can help you get it right, designing a retirement to make the remainder of your life more purposeful, productive, and fulfilling.

————————

Herminia Ibarra is the Charles Handy Professor of Organizational Behavior at London Business School and the author of *Working Identity* and *Act Like a Leader, Think Like a Leader* (both Harvard Business Review

Press, new editions forthcoming). Visit her website at herminiaibarra.com.

NOTES

1. Lindsay Jacobs and Suphanit Piyapromdee, "Labor Force Transitions at Older Ages: Burnout, Recovery, and Reverse Retirement," Finance and Economics Discussion Series 2016-053 (Washington, DC: Board of Governors of the Federal Reserve System, 2016), http://dx.doi.org/10.17016/FEDS.2016.053.

2. Mitra Toossi and Elka Torpey, "Older Workers: Labor Force Trends and Career Options," U.S. Bureau of Labor Statistics, May 2017, https://www.bls.gov/careeroutlook/2017/article/older-workers.htm.

3. "Longevity Economics: Leveraging the Advantages of an Aging Society," The Gerontological Society of America, https://www.geron.org/images/gsa/documents/gsa-longevity-economics-2018.pdf.

4. Will Kenton, "Reverse Retirement: Find Out Why So Many Retirees Are Going Back to Work," New Retirement, June 28, 2020, https://www.newretirement.com/retirement/reverse-retirement-find-out-why-retirees-are-going-back-to-work/; Riley Moynes, *The Four Phases of Retirement: What to Expect When You're Retiring*, audio book, (TMC Press, 2020).

5. Katharine G. Abraham, Brad Hershbein, and Susan N. Houseman, "Contract Work at Older Ages," Retirement and Disability Research Consortium, October 2019, https://www.nber.org/sites/default/files/2020-04/NB19-19a%20Abraham%2C%20Hershbein%20and%20Houseman%20GALLUP%20rev.pdf; "Older Entrepreneurs Own Half of U.S. Small Businesses, Bootstrap with Personal Savings, Credit Cards, and Retirement Funds," Cision, June 3, 2021 https://www.prnewswire.com/news-releases/older-entrepreneurs-own-half-of-us-small-businesses-bootstrap-with-personal-savings-credit-cards-and-retirement-funds-301305324.html; "Bridging Generational Divides to Co-Create the Future," Cogenerate, n.d., https://cogenerate.org/; "54% of Young Talent Desire a 'Portfolio Career,'" Talint International, November 30, 2021, https://www.talintinternational.com/54-of-young-talent-desire-a-portfolio-career/.

6. Laurie Quinn, "Going Back to College After 50: The New Normal?," *Forbes*, July 1, 2018, https://www.forbes.com/sites/nextavenue/2018/07/01/going-back-to-college-after-50-the-new-normal.

What Is Retirement Now?

CHAPTER 1

Next-Gen Retirement

by Heather C. Vough, Christine D. Bataille, Leisa Sargent, and Mary Dean Lee

Every day in the United States more than 10,000 people turn 65. For decades this was the typical retirement age. Starting in their early fifties, but certainly by age 70, people were expected to end their careers and embrace a life of leisure. But in the past 20 years, that paradigm has shifted dramatically. Half of today's 60-year-olds will live to at least age 90, according to Lynda Gratton and Andrew Scott, the authors of *The 100-Year Life*, which draws on the research of demographers Jim Oeppen and James Vaupel. Meanwhile, the era of corporate and

---

Reprinted from *Harvard Business Review*, June 2016 (product #R1606J).

government pension plans that promised lifetime financial security is over. For this and other reasons, many executives are now rethinking what it means to retire.

Researchers have spent a great deal of time investigating how organizations should respond to (and take advantage of) this trend. Indeed, an HBR article coauthored by Ken Dychtwald, an expert on aging, argued that companies should "retire retirement," keeping older workers engaged by creating cultures that value experience and allowing flexible schedules and exit plans.

In our work with executives, we've also become interested in how individuals are approaching 21st-century retirement. To explore the different paths being taken, we partnered with Jelena Zikic of York University to conduct in-depth interviews with 100 executives and managers who had recently retired or were actively considering it. We also interviewed HR professionals from 24 companies in the sectors where most of our study participants worked (financial services, natural resources, and high-tech manufacturing) to get a broader view of retirement today. We focused on managers because their departures have important organizational implications, and these people are more likely to have the financial means to make choices about when and how they retire.

We found much more variation in these individuals' opinions and experiences than traditional theories and clichés had led us to expect. In this article we summarize our findings. From the insights gathered, we've extrapolated four guiding principles that should help people of any generation navigate their late-career journeys: Prepare to go off-script; find your own retirement meta-phor; create a new deal; and make a difference.

Prepare to Go Off-Script

In listening to managers tell their stories, we discovered that very few had made a clear-cut, irrevocable shift from full-time work to retirement when they reached a certain age or eligibility. Their careers ended in many ways, often on unpredictable timetables. While some managers did describe "following the [traditional] script," others talked about "identifying a window" of opportunity when retirement felt right; "having an epiphany" because health or other events prompted a reorientation away from work; "cashing out" with a generous package; "becoming disillusioned" by organizational changes; and "being discarded"—essentially pushed out of a job or an organization. In sum, a number of factors influenced the way their retirements played out.

Consider Louis, 56, the general manager of a large division of an international telecommunications firm, who had spent 32 years at his company. He decided to retire earlier than expected when his employer appointed a man he didn't respect to be the new CEO. Although Louis stayed on for two years to help with a reorganization, he left as soon as he felt he could. Alan, 49, a successful and well-respected regional sales manager for a manufacturing company, had a similar story. After his firm changed ownership and was restructured, he was given three options: a lateral move involving geographical relocation, a demotion, or an early retirement package. Although he initially felt he was too young to retire, he decided it would be in his best interest to accept the package.

The lesson here is that few of us will have complete control over when and how our careers end, so we should all get ready to improvise and adapt. Mergers and acquisitions, shifts in management or strategic direction, restructurings, and unexpected personal events may not lead to an immediate exit, but they can set things in motion. No matter how well thought out your plan for retirement may be, there is a good chance that things won't turn out exactly as you'd hoped.

Find Your Retirement Metaphor

Managers use a variety of language when talking about retirement. Some think of it as *detox* from work stress, *liberation* from the daily grind, or *downshifting* from a demanding career (see table 1-1). Those metaphors all aptly describe the experiences of Jim, who retired from his position as the CEO of an international company when he was barely 50 because of a health scare. His father had died in his forties, and Jim didn't want to follow in his footsteps. Others envision a *renaissance* in their lives or a chance at *transformation*. Take Margaret, who stepped down from a demanding job in marketing and strategic planning at a consumer goods company to become an executive-in-residence at a prestigious business school. Still others regard retirement as a *milestone* in their career, worry about the *loss* of professional identity, or imagine *staying the course* and continuing to put their skills to use. A good example of the last is Bill, a geologist, who retired quite early from the oil company that had employed him for 25 years but soon decided to

TABLE 1-1

What does "retirement" mean to you?

Executives in their fifties and sixties use various metaphors to describe their post-career plans. Here are some of the most common:

Loss	A lack of purpose, a fear of being forgotten, or a threat to your identity
Renaissance	A new beginning, a new chapter, or a "blank canvas" offering possibilities to pursue your interests or passions
Detox	The "cleansing" experience of getting away from an unhealthy, stressful working life
Liberation	Being released from the constraints and restrictions of work; running toward a newfound freedom
Downshifting	Gaining time through the transition to a slower pace of life
Staying the course	Continued engagement and contribution; using your professional skills in different settings
Milestone	Reaching a pinnacle and achieving a goal; a marker of the end of one phase and the beginning of another
Transformation	A positive adaptation to a new role or lifestyle; taking on a new identity

Note: This table has been adapted from one the authors published in the *Journal of Vocational Behavior* in October 2011.

resume work by starting an oil-drilling venture with a colleague.

As people grow into retirement, however, their perspective on it often evolves. Some who initially see it as, say, liberation—the freedom to pursue golf or bridge or take cruises—can move into staying-the-course, transformation, or renaissance modes. Consider the rest of Jim's story. His first years of retirement were about unwinding and recovering from an all-consuming job, but he also began to miss aspects of his high-flying career. He first turned his attention to his family but eventually resumed a professional life coaching ambitious young managers.

In our research we found that individuals who take a flexible approach and are willing to shift from one metaphor to another are able to craft a retirement that feels right for them. So, especially if you're approaching this major life transition, take a moment to reflect on what it means to you. What images pop into your mind? Which, if any, of the metaphors we've described match your dreams and desires? If none of them resonate, is there another path for you? The idea is to better understand yourself, your perspectives on your work and your life, who you want to be going forward, and all the new activities or identities open to you.

Remember, too, that you can travel multiple paths in retirement. That versatility will be even more important for future generations. According to Gratton and Scott, people who are 20 years old today have a 50% chance of living to 100, while those who are 40 have the same odds of reaching 95. Even if you end your career at 75, you will probably want to try more than one type of retirement.

Create a New Deal

Rather than completely retiring, many professionals are striking deals to stay on at their organizations with re-designed schedules or responsibilities. Take Daniel, a senior executive at a financial institution who negotiated to continue his employment on a half-time basis. Now, for two weeks a month, he retreats to a fishing-and-hunting cabin in the coastal wilderness. But for the other two weeks, Daniel returns to corporate headquarters as a "thought leader" and mentor to up-and-coming executives. Another seasoned manager who participated in our study proposed a three-way job share with two colleagues who had young children. He wanted to step back but stay engaged; his coworkers wanted to keep developing their careers on family-friendly schedules; and their high-tech firm agreed to the plan.

Often executives take a phased retirement approach—gradually reducing their hours while helping to transfer knowledge and responsibility to their successors. For example, after reaching his pensionable retirement age, Mark, a senior forestry executive, negotiated to work on a 60% basis. That way, he could keep contributing to his company—in particular, by mentoring two teams of managers and helping with succession planning—but also respond to some pressing health issues. Over time he cut back his hours.

Another alternative is to arrange contract work with a former employer. Such deals benefit both the individuals (who receive compensation and the opportunity to reengage) and the organization (which can recapture lost expertise). Six months after Peter, a banker in his mid-fifties, retired, his former employer asked him to return on a contract basis to fill a role requiring his unique small-business-loan expertise.

Yet another exit path was taken by Adam, who in his early fifties requested a two-year leave of absence to serve as a city councilor. He returned to his firm for a time and then at age 56 formally retired from it, going on to lead a large community organization.

We encourage anyone considering retirement to explore different ways of staying or leaving. Take a hard look at what you do, at your unique experience, skills, and knowledge, and at how your employer views you. Reflect on the various roles you've had, projects you've completed, and where you've made the most meaningful contributions and felt most satisfied.

Not all organizations can facilitate innovative, one-off work roles or arrangements, but there may be more room to maneuver than you think. Once you have a good sense of the contribution you would like to make and your preferred schedule, broach the idea informally with your superiors or human resource managers. If they're unwilling to explore flexible options for staying on or transitioning out or to provide what you're looking for, consider reaching out to other organizations, which may be delighted to offer that flexibility.

Make a Difference

Retirement has long been seen as a time when people turn to philanthropic pursuits, perhaps following Andrew Carnegie's advice to spend the first third of your life getting educated, the second third getting rich, and the last third giving the money away. But we found that many of today's retirees are making much more than financial contributions to society. A few examples: After unexpectedly being fired in his early sixties, Harry, an engineer-turned-plant-manager in the pulp-and-paper industry, started working with high school dropouts to help them acquire marketable skills. Linda, a management training and development expert with 28 years of experience at a bank, retired at 50 and then went back to college to study international development with the intention of founding an orphanage for African children who'd lost their parents to AIDS. Sylvia, a successful investment banker close to burnout, retired early and took a big (unpaid) job as treasurer on the board of a major cultural institution. Gary, a telecommunications executive, left his position to launch a new venture to fund startups with social missions.

When you expect to live much longer, in better mental and physical health, the idea of shelving your expertise in retirement no longer makes sense. The new precedent—one that will no doubt be embraced by future generations, especially the socially conscious Millennials—is for retirees to leverage their knowledge, skill, and talent to make a difference in their communities or the world. Even if you're tired of the specific work you've been doing, your leadership, teamwork, and project management know-how can be applied to a host of other activities. Retirement is not an end but a beginning—an opportunity to experiment and explore, to engage in pursuits you value, and perhaps to reinvent your legacy.

———————

Heather C. Vough is an associate professor at George Mason University's School of Business. **Christine D. Bataille** is an associate professor at the Ithaca College School of Business. **Leisa Sargent** is dean, University of Sydney Business School. **Mary Dean Lee** is a professor emeritus in the Desautels Faculty of Management, McGill University.

CHAPTER 2

How Retirement Changes Your Identity . . . and Your Life

An interview with Teresa M. Amabile by Curt Nickisch

Health and wealth. Those two things are foremost in people's minds as they near the end of their working careers. *Can I afford to retire? Will I be healthy enough to enjoy it?* Research shows that when people are able to answer those two questions favorably, they're much happier in retirement. No surprise there.

Adapted from "How Retirement Changes Your Identity," *HBR IdeaCast* podcast, episode 665, January 15, 2019.

But there are other questions that people often find themselves asking after they've left the workplace for good. *Who am I now? When people ask me what I do, what do I even tell them?*

Work is such a huge part of our identity. Retirement untethers us from how we think of ourselves in a fundamental way. And a new study offers insights into how to handle this transition more effectively.

Researchers at Harvard Business School (Teresa Amabile), Questrom School of Business (Kathy Kram and Douglas T. Hall), Bentley University (Marcy Crary), and MIT Sloan School of Management (Lotte Bailyn) interviewed 120 professionals at three different companies across the United States.

In the study, they focused on the psychological, social, and relational shifts that retirement brings. And they found two key processes that retirement kicks off: life restructuring and identity bridging.

Teresa Amabile sat down with *HBR IdeaCast* host Curt Nickisch to talk about the study's findings. She's a semiretired professor at Harvard Business School and leads that team of researchers.

HBR: Was the fact that you were approaching retirement or in the midst of retirement a factor in your interest in doing this?

Teresa Amabile: Absolutely.

How so?

A few years ago, when I began conceiving of the research, my husband started telling friends that I wanted an evidence-based retirement for myself. And I guess it's true! Personally, I was very curious about how people approach it and what makes for a good retirement life.

I was also interested in retirement professionally, as an organizational behavior researcher focusing on how individuals experience work and life. My previous research discovered that people are happiest in their work on those days, weeks, and months when they feel that they're making progress in meaningful work.

What happens when you're leaving that meaningful work behind? Among my family, friends, and colleagues, there are some people who can't seem to leave their work behind. They don't want to make that transition.

It's almost like you're getting off a train, but at least a train has a sense of momentum or direction.

Exactly. Work has that sense of progress every day; even if it's a frustrating day, you usually made progress on something. And your metaphor of a train is interesting because you do feel like your life is moving you along and you know where that track is going.

You enter the unknown when you get off that train. And that can be very scary. There are some who get mired in that fear. And there are others who seem to be able to get on a new train or explore new trains. It seemed to me that those people were generally happier with their lives during the transition and in the immediate postretirement period.

Many people seem to take a lot of time to figure out what they want to do next.

In our research, we focused on the immediate pre-retirement period and the first five to seven years of retirement, especially the first year and a half. Some people start figuring out a new post-career life for themselves before they retire. That's unusual. The transition period to a more stable life can be pretty short—it can be a matter of a few months for those people. There are a couple of people that I followed for six years after they retired and, three years into it, one of them still felt like he didn't have a stable, settled retirement life.

It's counterintuitive because, on one hand, this is something you've known that you're going to do. People fantasize about retirement for decades. And then to say that three years into retirement, you're not really sure what you're doing or how you want to be spending your time. It seems like that should not be happening.

It's hard partly because a lot of our fantasizing has to do with finances. People certainly fantasize about not having the pressure or stress of work, but they also fantasize about not having to worry about money all the time. You know, if you've got your nest egg, then you imagine it will be smooth sailing. I don't think people realize *I've been doing something most of my waking hours for decades and I'm going to have to do something else during all those hours.*

So that's one of the two key processes that we've looked at in our research: life restructuring. You have to restructure your life that day you walk out of the office for the last time. Whether you've been working full- or part-time up to retirement, you're going to have to approach your life differently.

The other major process that we've discovered in our analyses is something we call *identity bridging*; it's a set of practices that people engage in that help them maintain important aspects of their self-identity across the retirement transition.

I want to ask about life restructuring first. In your research, you and your coauthors called it "being an architect." What does that mean?

Life structure is defined as the major contexts of your life—literally, the geographical, physical spaces where you spend your time, the major activities that you engage in, the most important relationships in your life.

When you're not working, a lot of that goes away.

We ask people who are retired, "Do you miss working?" Most say something like, "I don't miss the work, but I do miss the people." Most of us don't realize how anchoring and important those work relationships are.

We also don't realize how important the structure of work is. We have been living for several decades as a kind of tenant of a life structure that our organization has created for us. We know where we're going to be at 9 a.m. Monday through Friday, and we pretty much know what we're going to be doing and who we're going to be interacting with.

What we're going to eat . . .

What we're going to eat, where we're going to eat it. Because of the structure of that 9-to-5—or whatever the hours are—Monday through Friday, our weekends are also structured around that. Maybe one day or part of a day is when we do all the chores that we didn't have a chance for during the workweek.

One of our retirees said, "Well, you know, my life structure now is that I have Sunday—Church Day—followed by Saturday, Saturday, Saturday, Saturday, Saturday, Saturday."

Right, 300 Saturdays in a year.

Exactly. I can do whatever I want, and it's wonderful but also really unnerving. You have to think about where you're going to be spending your time and how you're going to structure that time. So there are four tasks that people have to go through in restructuring their lives. We call them *developmental tasks* because they're an important part of adult development for people who had a job through much of their lives.

The first one is *making the retirement decision.* That is a life structure decision—when to retire, how to retire. Do you want to get some kind of a part-time assignment at your workplace and gradually transition out? That's not just a decision about work though. It's also about your relationships, because many people—most in our study—are partnered. They have a spouse or a significant other who they share their life with.

You share a story in your research of the husband in a married couple who retires and comes home and alphabetizes the spices.

That was one of our favorite examples; the man said he drove his wife up the wall because she was the homemaker. That's the case with some baby boomer couples. She's got her own life structure, and suddenly it's being invaded by this person she hadn't spent significant weekday time with in maybe 30 or 40 years. Or ever.

This guy said, "I alphabetized all the spices the first day I was retired when she went off to her volunteer work. She said, 'You need to get out of this house for at least four hours every day.'" So they made a pact that he would be somewhere else. She didn't care where it was, just that he find something to do with himself.

So he found some volunteer work and made a regular breakfast date with friends in the neighborhood. But it took some negotiation with his partner. We're finding that in a lot of cases.

The second developmental task is *detaching from work*. For some, when they walk out that last day, it's like they're just taking off a backpack, setting it down, and walking away from it. For many people, it's not so easy.

Are they getting on the phone and calling people they worked with?

Yeah, or lurking on social media and trying to figure out what's going on at the office. Or they're still getting up at 5 a.m., and after breakfast, they're sitting down at their computer and going at email like they did when they were working.

Others have a hard time moving on psychologically. Even if they're not engaging in work activities, they're thinking about it a lot and feel that they're still in that world.

The third developmental task is *exploring and experimenting with a new, provisional retirement life structure*. This task is all about managing the liminal phase between feeling settled in a preretirement life and feeling settled in a postretirement life. Liminal means betwixt and between—in the midst of change of some kind. People have different strategies for approaching this. Some plan very carefully; others think up a number of possibilities without developing any definite plans. There's one person we interviewed who talked about a few ideas he was kicking around before his retirement date.

He felt very strongly that he had built great expertise, as a senior project leader in the company. He said, "You know, I think that I have something to give back by maybe writing a book about project management or possibly teaching a course on it."

Well, neither the book nor the teaching had happened by the time I last interviewed him, five years after he retired. What happened with the book and the course is what happens to many people that we've interviewed; he really liked being lazy after he retired.

I shouldn't use the word *lazy*, although some do use that word to describe themselves. We asked at the end of the interview, "What's the best thing about being retired so far for you?" A surprisingly large number of people say, without hesitation, "Not waking up to an alarm clock." And many others will say the best thing is the freedom, the flexibility to structure the day as they want.

Or not.

Or not. And they resist committing to something, especially something really ambitious—because that freedom just feels so good. Which brings up another of our findings: Almost everyone is very happy immediately after they retire, ranging from feeling very satisfied and content to feeling downright euphoric.

A huge, huge burden just goes away.

No commuting, which is enormous for many people. No stresses of another day where they haven't gotten everything done or have spent the day firefighting. Some enjoy that lack of structure so much that they find six months or even a year later, they're reluctant to do volunteer work that they absolutely intended to do and still do intend to do because it would require

29

them to give definite hours to the place and they
don't want to be tied down to that. But others really
need to have some structure to their days, soon after
that initial period of feeling like they're on vacation.
For example, one guy who was a cycling enthusiast
got himself a part-time job at a bicycle shop. He referred to it as his "landing spot" for when he made the
leap out of his career.

**One of the takeaways from this research is that you have
to think about what you want to do and not just get the
money equation solved. But even then it sounds like you
won't quite know what it's going to be like until you're
there because it's such a retraining of your brain.**

It is. Everything shifts. After the liminal phase is the
last of the four developmental tasks: *consolidating a
new, relatively stable life structure*. Many of the people
we interviewed had gotten to that point where they had
a new life structure that they were enjoying and felt
was really working. And there's no longer that sense of
urgency: I've got to get my life figured out. There was a
sense of being settled in a rhythm of life that felt right.

That's what we mean by the consolidation phase.
It can happen within a couple of months of retiring for some people. More often it's six months to a
year. In some cases, even three or four years later, the
person doesn't feel that they've quite got that new life
structure figured out.

For that reason, it's really great if a company has
a program where people can work part-time as they
transition to retirement.

That's what you're doing.

Yeah, that's what I'm doing. It's great because it allows you to experience that freedom and flexibility in many of your weekdays—not all your weekdays, but many of them.

You're not going cold turkey in some sense.

You're not going cold turkey, so you have a sense of what it's like to be at home on a day when you would normally be in your office. How do I want to interact with this other person who lives in the house? And do I want to try out some activities? We have many retirees in our study who did just relax and experience that freedom and flexibility for a few weeks or months—which can be a great way to begin retirement. And then they started talking to people at volunteer placements and getting involved in their communities, or they started getting more involved in something they'd enjoyed doing during their nonworking hours, before retirement, or they took the plunge into some new activity that had always beckoned to them. Often, wonderful new friendships grew from these activities.

But you found that for some people, it's been really, really difficult to transition to retirement because of those questions: Who am I? What am I doing? What am I good for?

Could I ask you one of the interview questions that we asked people in our study? Would you be more likely to say that your work is what you do or your work is who you are?

I would definitely be more likely to say that my work is who I am, and I have mixed feelings about that. If I look back on my career, I've probably been too slow to seize opportunities because I have felt a real strong identity in the role and with the company I was with.

In retrospect, I was exploiting myself more for the company than I should have. Some of this I think has to do with the way I grew up. My father was a career army officer, and I have a really strong sense of duty and doing what I'm supposed to do.

And maybe loyalty to that organization.

Yeah. And it's been a struggle to find the right balance.

Well, your very rich answer gives a little glimpse of how people think about their identity. For many of the people in our study—all professionals, knowledge workers—that identification with the work that they do or their profession or their organization or their colleagues is very strong.

What do you do with that? What do you do with that big chunk of yourself as you retire? We've discovered that many people engage in what we call *identity bridging*—by which I mean somehow maintaining or enhancing an important aspect of yourself that existed preretirement. Our findings suggest that, if you did identify strongly with your work, if it was a big piece of who you were, you're better off if you can do some identity bridging. One important way in which some people do that is to actually bridge a piece of the worker identity.

So this is working for a nonprofit and volunteering.

Exactly, that's one way to do it. For one person we interviewed, being a leader in his company had been an important aspect of his work identity. He bridged that identity and brought it into his postretirement life by taking on a volunteer leadership role in the church where he'd long been a member. He found this immensely satisfying and, as a retiree, he happily used the word "leader" when we asked him to give us a few descriptors of his core identity.

Other people might bridge their work identity by starting up their own one-person consulting firm as they're retiring, as one of our interviewees did. Her last role in her organization before retiring was to coach new employees. She loved that so much that she considered it her calling—a calling discovered relatively late in her career. So she decided to focus her postretirement, part-time consulting business on coaching young managers and entrepreneurs.

A few other people in our study started entre-preneurial ventures. The worker identity had been central for one such person, and he dreaded going from full-time work to nothing. Many people referred to this as "leaping off the cliff" or "jumping into the void." That's how scary it can be. This person started a handyman business after he retired. He had loved fixing things around the house when he was in his career as a high-level tech person. He thought, "You know what? I can do this for neighbors and friends and for people in the community."

So he actually created a little LLC. He printed up business cards. He wasn't charging much, and he wasn't spending a lot of hours a week doing this. But when people asked him what he did, he was able to avoid saying what he dreaded, which was, "Well, I'm retired." He was able to say, "Oh, I've got a handyman business. Let me give you my card." And having that tangible object was really important for him. It was like anchoring that worker identity with a tangible thing.

For other people, the important identity bridging across the retirement transition isn't about their work identity. It's about enhancing or developing some nonwork aspect of identity that they had while they were still working. One of the most common things we've seen is that people have had an avocation that they enjoyed preretirement and then they get much more intensely engaged in it after retirement. For example, one person who enjoyed playing guitar joined a band after retiring—and soon developed a fuller identity as a musician. That kind of identity bridging can be very fulfilling and enjoyable. Sometimes a retiring person will focus on a relationship they had preretirement that formed an important part of their identity—and they're now deepening that engagement, spending more time with that person.

For example, we had a retiree who talked about how his father identity had always been important to him. He had three kids, and one was still at home when he retired. She was an older teenager in high school and was struggling a bit with her schoolwork and a few other aspects of her life. They had a close relationship, but they didn't spend much time together when he was working because his career just sucked up all the air in his life.

He became much more engaged with her after retiring. He helped her with her schoolwork. They did projects together. So that really enriched his life, and it bridged that father identity, which had been a small but important part of his identity before. Now it occupied a very big piece of his identity.

You also talk about people who bring up stuff from their past, like somebody who loved hot rods when he was younger and then bought one as he was about to retire. It's the classic retirement project, right?

Yes! We call that *activating a dormant identity*. This person had been an avid hot-rodder until the pressures of work and moving up the corporate ladder took over. Also, early in his career, his wife begged him, saying, "Look, we've got young children. You're engaging in something dangerous. Please don't go out on those hot rod races."

So he sold his hot rod. Then as he was approaching retirement, he bought a new one.

What have I got to lose?

Yes. His wife said, "Go for it, baby." He loved getting reengaged with the hot rod community, going out

35

on group rides. That was a beautiful identity bridge for him.

In many cases, it's about waking those things up. I wonder if this is a failure of corporate America though, because you talk about climbing the corporate ladder taking all the oxygen, right? Or people just not having time for that. Sure, you can do a better job preparing for retirement, but is it also the way that companies expect people to work for them that means they don't really know who they are when they're done working?

Absolutely. So much of our identity is almost necessarily wrapped up in our work. So much of our mind space is occupied by our work that we let other pieces of ourselves atrophy. For myself, my cooking skills have completely atrophied, in part because I have a wonderful husband who's a gourmet cook, and his career was less demanding than mine.

Something interesting we've seen in our interviewees is that, if people can maintain some creative activity outside of work, even while they're fully engaged in their career, that seems to stand them in good stead because it's something they can grow afterward. It gives them a natural identity bridge.

How have you changed your plans for retirement, based on this research?

Not only have I been allowing myself to spend time on this research, which I love, but I've also been allowing myself to allocate some time each week to my avocations—one of which is being a grandmother.

Another avocation of mine is literature. I've been reading more poetry and trying my hand at writing more. I've also been deepening my relationships with my husband, our daughter, and my five sisters. That's all enriched me incredibly.

When you retire, what will you tell people you do?

I'll tell them I'm a retired professor from Harvard Business School, and I'll tell them what else I'm doing at that time.

––––––––––––

Teresa M. Amabile is a Baker Foundation Professor at Harvard Business School and the coauthor of *The Progress Principle*. Her current research, which she and her coresearchers are writing a book about, investigates how people approach and experience the transition to retirement. **Curt Nickisch** is a senior editor at *Harvard Business Review*, where he makes podcasts and cohosts *HBR IdeaCast*. He earned an MBA from Boston University and previously reported for NPR, *Marketplace*, WBUR, and *Fast Company*. He speaks *ausgezeichnet* German and binges history podcasts.

Define Retirement for Yourself

CHAPTER 3

Design a Retirement That Excites You

by Jeff Giesea

When George Thorne walks into his medical practice in Austin, Texas, he is greeted warmly by staff and makes friendly conversation about kids and pets. An ophthalmologist for 30-plus years, he is quick to speak fondly of his patients, medical partners, and team. It's clear he has loved his career. But at age 65, he recently decided to stop performing surgery and phase himself out of his practice altogether. "I'm not sure what's on the other

Adapted from content posted on hbr.org, November 17, 2015 (product #H02I1Q).

side of this," he told me with a hint of anguish, "but it's time."

George is like many of the baby boomers I work with in my executive coaching practice. They've had high-powered careers that they've found fulfilling and are core to their identities. As they approach so-called retirement age, they are ready (or forced) to transition out of their longtime professions and are somewhat anxious about what's next. Their concerns are less financial than identity- and change-related: *How can I successfully reinvent myself as I leave behind my career? What does the next phase look like for me? How can I make sure I don't get bored?*

I once joked with my friend Aaron: "If you want to provoke a baby boomer, ask them about retirement." Many boomers are allergic to the R-word. The reasons are understandable. Retirement, for many, implies a binary off-switch toward mortality, golf, and bingo. It suggests a fixed destination when the 21st-century reality is much more fluid and personalized.

So rather than framing this work as planning for retirement, I encourage people like George to think of it as designing your next phase. This isn't just a cute turn of phrase. Positioning it this way, I find, creates a more empowered process. It shifts the tone by broadening the range of possibilities, by making it feel evolutionary rather than final, and by reinforcing that they are in the driver's seat. It's also more fun. *This is a reinvention you get to design, not a retirement you have to plan.*

Here are some tips that can help make designing your next phase a smoother and more fulfilling experience.

Name it

One of the first things I ask people in this situation is what they want to call it. What word should we use when we talk about it? Some stick with retirement. Others come up with thematic names like "encore career," "play time," or "giving back."

My friend Craig left his post as CIO of a *Fortune* 100 company two years ago after a successful, international corporate career. At 63, he no longer works in the traditional sense, but he doesn't consider himself retired either. He spends his time advising early-stage startups and helping out political campaigns, in addition to travel and family. When I ask him what he calls this chapter of his life, he says, "It's my repurposing phase." For Craig, "repurposing phase" is better than "retirement" because staying engaged and making a difference are important to him in this chapter. "I like having people call me on the phone," he said. "I want to feel like I'm still relevant."

Naming the next chapter is the first step in taking control over it, of making it yours. It might feel like a cheap obfuscation, but in fact it's the opposite. By naming it using your language, you bring clarity to what this next phase means to you. The name doesn't have to make sense to everybody. It just has to make sense to you.

Give yourself time to shed old skin

Two weeks ago, an executive vice president called to tell me that she had just been let go after a merger. "They told me yesterday," she said. "I don't what I'm going to do next. Maybe it's time to retire. I don't know."

"I wonder if it might help to take some time to process this before figuring out what's next," I replied. "Why don't you go hiking or something, and let's talk in a couple weeks." Yesterday I got an email from her from the mountains of Oregon. She took my advice literally! "I didn't realize how much I needed this," she wrote.

When people step away from a high-octane career, many want to power through the change. It's as if they believe a swirl of activity, or some dramatic new commitment, will alleviate the sense of loss and disorientation that comes with stepping off the treadmill.

Instead, allow time and space to land from the experience, to shed the old skin. Recognize that there will be a grieving process for your old identity. It's not like flipping a switch and suddenly being in a sunny new chapter; you will go through different stages. (See the sidebar "4 Questions to Help You Plan Your Retirement—or Your Next Act" to help you think about possibilities.)

Craig, mentioned above, gave himself six months "with no pressure to be productive" when he left his CIO role. "It was one of the best things I did," he said. He knew there would be a process of shedding his old identity and allowed himself space to recover.

Envision your new world

One tool I find helpful in transitions is the "wheel of life." This wheel looks like a pie with eight slices representing different elements of life: Fun, Health, Money, Friends, Career, Spouse, Physical Environment (home), and Personal Growth. A useful exercise is to go through each category and write out your vision for each. Where are

4 QUESTIONS TO HELP YOU PLAN YOUR RETIREMENT—OR YOUR NEXT ACT

by Dorie Clark

Here are four key questions to consider as you're planning your retirement—or your reinvention.

How much money do you need to earn?

If earning a certain amount of money is mandatory for your retirement plans, that criterion comes first, and will likely limit your options. Specifically, you're more likely to need to continue working full-time (since those positions are usually more remunerative), and you may need to stick close to the field in which you spent the bulk of your career, because you'll get paid more for the seniority and experience you've accrued. If earning a robust salary isn't mandatory, however, there are other questions to consider.

How much location independence do you want?

If you have visions of balancing a little bit of work with a lot of travel, or you'd like to winter in sunny climes, you'll want to think about how to cultivate a location-independent retirement. Perhaps you choose a job that only operates for a portion of the year and allows flexibility the rest of the time (such as being a teacher or university instructor). Or you may want to focus on jobs that can be done from anywhere (such as a freelance writer or consultant), or companies that offer remote or hybrid options. As long as you have a deep

(continued)

**4 QUESTIONS TO HELP YOU PLAN YOUR
RETIREMENT—OR YOUR NEXT ACT**

network of contacts to land the work in the first place, it may not matter where you're based when you're actually performing it.

How radical a change are you seeking?

If you're still interested in your current field, but would simply like to downshift, you have some easy options. One is to discuss the possibility with your current employer of transitioning from a full-time employee into a consultant role, perhaps working a few days a week, or focusing on a specific project. That can ease your transition into retirement with a guaranteed paycheck before you walk out the door. Alternatively, you may have other industry contacts that would like to hire you as a consultant. If you're looking for a bolder change and to leave your current field behind, you'll need to start laying the groundwork early because you're likely to have fewer contacts in your new profession.

How can you start test-driving your future career now?

In my book *Reinventing You*, I profile a woman named Patricia Fripp, who started her career as a hairdresser but discovered that she loved public speaking. She honed her skills on the side initially, doing presentations at hair shows; eventually some of her haircutting clients who worked for corporations invited her to present on customer service and sales to their teams. But despite her passion for speaking, she knew it would be rash to quit her day job and try to make a living from it right away. Instead, she had a 10-year lease on her hair salon, and she created a long-term plan to build up her book of speaking business so that when her lease expired, she could transition seamlessly into her new profession—and that's what she did. The further in advance you start planning, the more runway you have to experiment and try out new directions on the side, while you still have the security of your regular income.

Many people want—or need—to keep working in retirement, ideally taking on an interesting, personal growth opportunity. By asking yourself these questions, and starting to plan for your next act as soon as possible, you can ease your transition into your next meaningful challenge.

———————

Dorie Clark is a marketing strategist and keynote speaker who teaches at Duke University's Fuqua School of Business and has been named one of the Top 50 business thinkers in the world by Thinkers50. Her latest book is *The Long Game: How to Be a Long-Term Thinker in a Short-Term World* (Harvard Business Review Press, 2021)

Adapted from "Planning Your Post-Retirement Career," on hbr.org, April 28, 2016 (product #H02UFU).

you now in this area, and where might you like to take these in your transition? If you have a spouse or partner, involve them in the process. Reinventions are a team sport, after all.

Another simple but surprisingly powerful exercise is to take a sheet of paper and draw your life in three years. If you don't like to draw, create vision boards instead. Spending some time visioning will create new neural pathways, allow you to try on different visions of your life, and can help tease out the things that are important to you (and your partner, if you have one).

Embrace experiments

As with any design process, prototyping is a useful way to see what works and what doesn't. If you're thinking of moving to a beach in Florida, rent a place there for two weeks and try it out. If you want to do volunteer work with refugees, go network with people in that world and consider taking a two-week trip to a refugee camp. If you want to write the great American novel, take a first step by joining a local writers' group.

Some people are uneasy with the uncertainty and in-between-ness of not having a firm plan. For those who crave structure, I recommend picking two or three specific things to explore, setting a specific time period for this phase, and then creating a calendar of activity. Think of it this way: Your new job is to prototype these two or three specific interests or possibilities.

If you're worried about what to say when people ask what you do, just mention the work you did in the past and the two or three new areas you're investigating.

Don't want to give up business cards? That's fine. Order personal cards printed with your name and contact info—they don't have to have a job title.

Stake out a new purpose and routine

Routines are healthy; one of my favorite sayings is that "structure sets you free." But it's tough to stick to a routine when you don't have a purpose. (And conversely, routine without purpose is dull.)

And yet as people go through these transitions, there's often a period when they haven't settled into either a new purpose or a new routine. This can feel hollow, and drive those around you a little crazy. This is normal. In fact, there's something healthy about a nagging ennui during a major reinvention. But eventually, you will want to create new routines and a sense of purpose for yourself, even if it initially feels contrived.

If you have planning time before a transition, I strongly recommend preparing at least one new "identity" or interest area in advance. A law partner I know, for example, is getting credentialed as a mediator to get ready for his retirement in two years. Another person I know is developing a relationship with a local university in anticipation of teaching a course. These may or may not work out, but they can create some initial structure.

A longtime mentor of mine, Charles, is a retired PR executive who splits his time between Alaska and Washington, DC. Charles once told me that the arc of life is: Learn-Earn-Serve. At 66, Charles has found purpose in this stage of life through what he calls "archive activism." He founded the Kameny Papers Projects, a collection of historical documents associated with Frank Kameny, whom he describes as the Rosa Parks of the LGBTQ+ movement. For Charles, this focus was an evolution of interests over time. Eventually, he embraced it.

To thrive in this next phase, you will need a reason to jump out of bed in the morning. It doesn't matter what it is, it just has to resonate with you and your values.

Take small steps toward designing this next phase— not just financially, but as a whole person and family. You have the power to make it the most fulfilling and joyful period of your life.

––––––––––

Jeff Giesea is an entrepreneur and executive coach based in Florida.

CHAPTER 4

What Surviving Pandemic Lockdowns Can Teach Us About Major Life Changes

by Herminia Ibarra

Many of us believe that unexpected events or shocks create fertile conditions for major life and career changes by sparking us to reflect about our desires and priorities. That holds true for the coronavirus pandemic. When I asked people in an online poll to tell me how the pandemic had affected their plans for career change,

Adapted from "The 3 Phases of Making a Major Life Change," on hbr .org, August 6, 2021 (product #H06HXJ).

51

49% chose this response: "It has given me downtime to rest and/or think."

That's a good start, especially for those of us nearing the end of our working lives, where often we're too busy to consider what lies ahead. But if there is one thing, I have learned from decades of studying successful career change, it's that *thinking* on its own is far from sufficient. We rarely think our way into a new way of acting. Rather, we act our way into new ways of thinking—and being.

Yes, events that disrupt our habitual routines have the potential to catalyze real change. They give us a chance to experiment with new activities and to create and renew connections. Even in the seemingly unproductive time we spend away from our everyday work lives, we conduct important inner business—asking the big existential questions, remembering what makes us happy, shoring up the strength to make difficult choices, consolidating our sense of self, and more.[1]

Enough happened during the pandemic to make many of us keenly aware of what we no longer want. But the problem is this: More appealing, feasible alternatives may have yet to materialize. So we're stuck in limbo between old and new. And, with Covid restrictions falling away and a return to the office and regular pace of life, we confront a real danger: getting sucked back into our former jobs and ways of working.

How can those of us who want to make a career transition avoid that? How can we make progress toward our goals by building on what we learned in the lockdown?

Research on the transformative potential of a catalyzing event like the coronavirus pandemic suggests that we are more likely to make lasting change when we actively engage in a three-part cycle of transition—one that gets us to focus on *separation*, *liminality*, and *reintegration*. Let's consider each of those parts of the cycle in detail.

The Benefits of Separation

"I spent lockdown in this idyllic, secluded environment," I was told by John, a businessman whose last executive role came to an end around the onset of the pandemic, enabling him to move out into the country. "I got to see the spring come and go," he said. "I got to see a lot of nature. It was just an amazingly peaceful backdrop. I got married last year, so my wife and I had an enormous amount of time together. My son, from whom I'd been estranged, came to stay with us. So I got to know him again, which was a great experience. This was a very blessed period."

John's experience wasn't unique. Research on how moving can facilitate behavior change suggests that people who found a new and different place to live during the pandemic may have better chances of making life changes that stick.[2] Why? Because of what's known as "habit discontinuity."[3] We are all more malleable when separated from the people and places that trigger old habits and old selves.[4]

Change always starts with separation. Even in some of the ultimate forms of identity change—brainwashing, de-indoctrinating terrorists, or rehabilitating substance abusers—the standard operating practice is to separate subjects from everybody who knew them previously, and to deprive them of a grounding in their old identities. This separation dynamic explains why young adults change when they go away to college and why older adults change when they retire from their professional lives.

My recent research has shown how much our work networks are prone to the "narcissistic and lazy" bias.[5] The idea is this: We are drawn spontaneously to, and maintain contact with, people who are similar to us (we're narcissistic), and we get to know and like people whose proximity makes it easy for us to get to know and like them (we're lazy).

The pandemic disrupted at least physical proximity for most of us. But that might not be enough to mitigate the powerful similarities that the narcissistic and lazy bias create for us at work. That's why maintaining some degree of separation from the network of relationships that defined our former professional lives can be vital to our reinvention, at any stage.

Tammy English of Washington University and Laura Carstensen of Stanford University found that the size of people's networks shrank after the age of 60, not because these people had fewer opportunities to connect but because, increasingly, they perceived time as being limited, which made them more selective.[6] Quite possibly many of our experiences of the pandemic, like John's, will foster our reinvention by encouraging greater selectivity in how and with whom we spend our limited time.

Liminal Learnings

When the pandemic hit, Sophie, a former lawyer, was transitioning out of a two-decade career and found herself wanting to explore a range of new work possibilities, among them documentary filmmaking, journalism, nonexecutive board roles, and sustainability consulting. Lockdown created a liminal time and space, a "betwixt and between" zone, in which the normal rules that governed Sophie's professional life were temporarily lifted, and she felt able to experiment with all sorts of work and leisure pursuits without committing to any of them. She made the most of that period—taking several courses, working on startup ideas, doing freelance consulting, joining a nonprofit board, and producing two of her first short films.

Taking advantage of liminal interludes allows us to experiment—to do new and different things with new and different people. In turn, that affords us rare opportunities to learn about ourselves and to cultivate new knowledge, skills, resources, and relationships. But these interludes don't last forever. At some point, we have to cull learning from our experiments and use it to take some informed next steps in our plans for change. What is worth pursuing further? What new interest has cropped up that's worth a look? What will you drop having learned that it's not so appealing after all? What do you keep, but only as a hobby?

When Sophie took stock, she was surprised to realize that she hadn't grown in her board role as much as she had expected, whereas she had very quickly started to build meaningful connections linked to the film industry. These were vital recognitions for her to make before she committed herself to next steps in her transition plan.

Reintegration: A Time for New Beginnings

Most of the executives and professionals with whom I have exchanged pandemic experiences tell me that they do not want to return to hectic travel schedules or long hours that sacrifice time with their families—but are nonetheless worried that they will.

They are right to be worried, because external shocks rarely produce lasting change. The more typical pattern after we receive some kind of wake-up call is simply to revert back to form once things return to "normal." That's what Wharton professor Alexandra Michel found when she investigated the physical consequences of overwork for four cohorts of investment bankers over a 12-year period.[7] For these people, avoiding unsustainable work habits required more than changing jobs or even occupations. Many of them had physical breakdowns even after moving into organizations that were supposedly less work intensive. Why? Because they had actually moved into similarly demanding positions, but without taking sufficient time in between roles to convalesce and gain psychological distance from their hard-driving selves.

Our ability to take advantage of habit discontinuity depends on what we do in the narrow window of opportunity that opens up after routine-busting changes. One study has found, for example, that the window of opportunity for engaging in more environmentally sustainable behaviors lasts up to three months after people move house.[8] Similarly, research on the "fresh start" effect shows that while people experience heightened goal-oriented motivation after returning to work from a holiday, this motivation peaks on the first day back and declines rapidly thereafter.[9]

It's up to you to decide whether what you learned in the pandemic effected real change in your professional life—or whether, instead, you'll drift back into your old job and patterns as if nothing ever happened.

Herminia Ibarra is the Charles Handy Professor of Organizational Behavior at London Business School and the author of *Working Identity* and *Act Like a Leader, Think Like a Leader* (both Harvard Business Review Press, new editions forthcoming). Visit her website at herminiaibarra.com.

NOTES

1. M. H. Immordino-Yang, J. A. Christodoulou, and V. Singh, "Rest Is Not Idleness: Implications of the Brain's Default Mode for Human Development and Education," *Perspectives on Psychological Science* 7, no. 4 (2012): 352–364.

2. Bas Verplanken and Deborah Roy, "Empowering Interventions to Promote Sustainable Lifestyles: Testing the Habit Discontinuity Hypothesis in a Field Experiment," *Journal of Environmental Psychology* 45 (2016): 127–134.

3. Verplanken and Roy, "Empowering Interventions."

4. Lucas Carden and Wendy Wood, "Habit Formation and Change," *Current Opinion in Behavioral Sciences* 20 (2018): 117–122.

5. H. Ibarra, "Five Leadership Skills for the Future," *Leader to Leader*, June 18, 2021, 14–17.

6. T. English and L. L. Carstensen, "Selective Narrowing of Social Networks Across Adulthood Is Associated with Improved Emotional Experience in Daily Life," *International Journal of Behavioral Development* 38, no. 2 (2014): 195–202.

7. Alexandra Michel, "Dualism at Work: The Social Circulation of Embodiment Theories in Use," *Signs and Society* 3, no. 1 (2015): S41–S69.

8. Verplanken and Roy, "Empowering Interventions."

9. Hengchen Dai, Katherine L. Milkman, and Jason Riis, "The Fresh Start Effect: Temporal Landmarks Motivate Aspirational Behavior," *Management Science* 60, no. 10 (2014): 2563–2582.

CHAPTER 5

How to Craft a Better Retirement

by Rob Baker

What does a positive retirement look and feel like? The answer will be different for everyone, but a successful and smooth retirement transition involves so much more than financial planning. Along with investing in your pension pot, you need to invest from a personal and professional perspective.

Whether your runway to retirement is long or short, job crafting—personalizing how you do, and think about, your job—is a powerful way of maximizing your impact at work in the final stage of your career. It can help you nurture the skills, experiences, and connections that will serve you as you start your next life adventure. In practice, this means finding ways to use your strengths and passions to shape your work around your current needs and future ambitions. This might include amplifying or dialing down aspects of your job that you love or loathe; pursuing new opportunities; and changing or downshifting your work commitments as you plan for a (literal) full stop.

The term "job crafting" was first coined by two researchers, Amy Wrzesniewski and Jane Dutton.[1] In a study involving hospital cleaners, they found that certain employees actively personalized their jobs rather than just adhering to their job descriptions. In the time since their research was first published, many more studies have shown the power of job crafting for employees worldwide, ranging from chefs to chief executives. These studies show that positive things happen when we deliberately tailor our work, including fostering performance, well-being and thriving, and personal and professional growth.[2]

Why Is Preretirement the Perfect Time to Start Personalizing Your Work?

Perhaps counterintuitively, the end of your career can be the perfect time to start crafting. Through my practice and research helping hundreds of individuals and teams to job craft (detailed in my book *Personalization at Work*), I have found that people in the later phases of their professional lives often have the confidence and credibility to shape their work—and greater clarity about what they want from their jobs and lives, compared with their younger professional selves.

Job crafting allows us to create and maintain a positive "person-job fit," meaning there is alignment and harmony between our personal needs and motivations and the work we do.[3] Maintaining this fit can be particularly important in the latter stages of our careers as our psychological, physical, and professional requirements often change. We may, for example, have parental caring responsibilities to juggle or less energy (or patience) for evening networking. Or we may have an increased interest in our passions or a desire to create a positive and lasting legacy at work. Job crafting allows us to shape our work around our new and evolving needs.

There are plenty of unfair and outdated assumptions about people approaching retirement age disengaging from work and personal development. It may also be a bias we hold against ourselves—why learn that new platform or add new colleagues to our network if we anticipate leaving our company in five years? Experimenting with job crafting can serve as a counterpoint. It signals that you are still proactively learning and changing, rather than coasting toward the finish line. Job crafting can help you tick off items on your professional bucket list in a positive and proactive way. It allows you to develop and maintain a growth mindset, consciously uncouple with your work on your terms, and buffer the feelings of being untethered and unconnected that the recently retired often report.[4]

Engaging in job crafting can also help you set yourself up for success after retirement. With seven in 10

Americans planning to work during their retirement, job crafting could create or strengthen opportunities for new work; side hustles are not just for those entering the workforce.[5]

What Job Crafting Your Retirement Plans Might Look Like for You

Just like people (and their retirement plans), job crafting comes in different shapes and sizes. While the way employees customize their jobs differs from person to person, there are five core ways to use job crafting in retirement related to tasks, skills, well-being, relationships, and purpose.

Task crafting

Task crafting involves changing the boundaries of your job by adding or removing tasks or finding ways to dial up or down aspects that you love or loathe. You can restructure how you organize your day and improve workflow processes and systems, or how you run meetings.

Take Ian, a structural engineer in his early sixties. He wanted to find ways to contribute to his organization's future, so he volunteered to take a more active role in his company's graduate recruitment and internal promotions programs by chairing and sitting on selection panels. While Ian previously resisted such activities to prioritize client work (and, yes, his billable hours), at this point in his career, he is more motivated to be a positive corporate citizen. Adding these tasks to his role allows Ian to find a new way to use his technical knowledge and experience. He will feel more settled and satisfied when he retires, knowing he has invested some time in supporting the success of others and his own progression.

Skill crafting

Skill crafting is about growing as an individual, perhaps by deepening your skills and knowledge in certain areas or learning new things.

Examples of late-career skill crafting include sharpening your financial planning skills to support your preparations for retirement or undertaking specific coaching and mentoring training. Brian, an advertising executive, started an industry blog, sharing his insights and predictions on trends and news, developing his writing skills, and setting himself up for success as a conference speaker in retirement.

Well-being crafting

Well-being crafting involves shaping how you do your work to make it healthier from a mental or physical perspective. The significance that mental and physical well-being plays in retirement satisfaction is well known, but you don't have to wait until retirement to nurture well-being habits.[6]

John, a chief information officer at a university, practiced well-being crafting by actively phasing down his habit of working on weekends. On the brink of burnout, John realized that he needed to find new ways to reenergize. In the past he had tried and failed to simply go cold turkey and avoid emails on the weekends but found himself feeling lost and anxious. The answer for John involved reigniting a past passion for photography. He found that setting photography challenges on a Sunday morning brought him more focus (and fun) than answering emails. While he still allowed himself to open his inbox in the evening, over time he said he had less desire to do so. John knew that taking photos could have a positive influence in the next phase of his life; he had already eyed photography groups in his local area that he was thinking of joining once he had more free time.

Relationship crafting

Relationship crafting involves shaping the way we engage with people we interact with at work, including colleagues, clients, and customers. This includes building new connections, amplifying existing ones, or consolidating and changing current connections.

Lisa, a chief people officer at a nonprofit, crafted relationships by getting more involved in the activities of a regional branch of the CIPD (the U.K.'s national HR professional body). She had two motivations for growing her connections: First, she enjoyed meeting new people, and second, she knew this network could support her postretirement plans to offer executive coaching to emerging HR leaders.

Another example is Alice, who led a bank's customer services team. She shared that she was deliberately disengaging, or doing her best to limit interactions, with certain colleagues she said were "mood hoovers": people who suck the life out of you. With only a few years of working left, she told me that "life was too short" to volunteer for projects or attend social events involving people she didn't like. (Go Alice!) This no-nonsense approach to relationships would serve her well in postretirement when navigating which friendship groups and different clubs and committees she wanted to spend more (or less) of her time with.

Purpose crafting

You can craft a purpose by changing or reshaping how you think about aspects of work that you find meaningful, purposeful, and in alignment with your values and by finding ways to prioritize and foster elements of your job that serve your personal and professional sense of purpose.

Management consultancy partner Jane was struggling with the idea of turning over client accounts when she retired, given how invested she was in these relationships. By considering her purpose and actively reframing this activity, she recognized that a positive transfer was the best way to serve her clients for the future—something that aligned with her values. She strove to savor the handover, seeing transition meetings as an opportunity to reflect and reminisce about the successes (and scrapes) she and her clients had seen together.

An Exercise to Help You Craft Your Retirement

Job crafting involves creating space and having the energy to be curious about how you do your work and finding ways to improve it—just like an athlete working with a coach to break down and improve their running form. Questions to prompt reflections at work include thinking about how, when, and why you do your job.

The following past, future, and present exercise can help you identify opportunities to craft a positive retirement. You can write down your answers, think about them on a walk, talk them through with a friend or partner, or even draw pictures and sketch notes to represent your answers.

You don't have to have a specific job-crafting focus or type in mind when completing this activity; the first two stages of the exercise will guide you toward a job-crafting goal that will have relevance and resonance for you.

- **Past.** What elements of work have energized you most in the past? What achievements are you most proud of? What pieces of feedback have you most valued?

  Your answers to these questions will give you insights into the types of work you should find or hold onto as you head toward retirement and beyond. For example, if you value and enjoy working in groups, using your professional expertise and leadership experience, you might explore post-retirement opportunities that value these attributes, such as committee, trustee, or nonexecutive director roles.

- **Future.** How do you want to feel when you retire? What do you want to be excited about? What do you want your legacy to be? What do you want others to say about you at your retirement party? What relationships do you want to maintain, and which ones do you look forward to severing?

  This twist on the traditional future-work self-exercise—often used at the start of our careers—

will help you identify what a positive retirement looks like and help you to orient your current work in that direction.[7]

- **Present.** Now it's time to craft your current job to align with your future aspirations, holding onto what matters to you.

The secret to job crafting is to start small and consider it a form of playful experimentation. As a coach, I often give individuals and groups a crafting budget of 10 minutes a day, or an hour a week, to find the smallest and most positive ways to make their current job 1% better. I encourage people to select a type of job crafting that most motivates and speaks to them at that time and then identify an opportunity to do this.

A small skill-crafting experiment could involve spending the first 10 minutes of your lunch break learning Italian with an app, for a long-planned postretirement trip. You could foster well-being by blocking out an hour once a week to go to the gym (and boost your chance of success by asking your team to keep you accountable) or craft a purpose by volunteering to get involved in something you care about at work, such as mentoring future leaders (within your organization or your wider professional field).

A thriving retirement is something you build, not something that just happens. Approaching retirement job crafting with curiosity and commitment enables you to start shifting your work in a positive direction, making it more enjoyable and stimulating in the present and more rewarding once you log off for the final time. It can help focus on the things that matter to you and put you in control as you transition into this new phase.

It's time to bring a personal touch to your retirement plans. By crafting the job you have today, you can set yourself up for the retirement you want tomorrow.

———————————

Rob Baker is the founder and Chief Positive Deviant of Tailored Thinking, an award-winning HR consultancy with the mission to be a force for good in the world of work using positive psychology and well-being science. Rob is the author of *Personalization at Work*; his work and research on bringing job crafting to life has been presented at academic and professional conferences around the globe. Rob's TEDx talk "The Power of Personalizing Our Work" was released in 2021. Prior to Tailored Thinking, he held leadership roles at the University of Melbourne and the University of Sheffield and is a Chartered Fellow of the CIPD and Australian HR Institute.

NOTES

1. A. Wrzesniewski and J. E. Dutton, "Crafting a Job: Revisioning Employees as Active Crafters of Their Work," *Academy of Management Review* 26, no. 2 (2001): 179–201, https://asset-pdf.scinapse.io/prod/2113953571/2113953571.pdf.

2. R. Baker, *Personalization at Work: How HR Can Use Job Crafting to Drive Performance, Engagement and Wellbeing* (London: Kogan Page Publishers, 2020); P. W. Lichtenthaler and A. Fischbach, "A Meta-Analysis on Promotion- and Prevention-Focused Job Crafting," *European Journal of Work and Organizational Psychology*, 28, no. 1 (2019): 30–50.

3. C. M. Wong and L. E. Tetrick, "Job Crafting: Older Workers' Mechanism for Maintaining Person-Job Fit," *Frontiers in Psychology* 8 (2017): 1548, https://www.frontiersin.org/articles/10.3389/fpsyg.2017.01548/full.

4. G. Topa and E. Valero, "Preparing for Retirement: How Self-Efficacy and Resource Threats Contribute to Retirees' Satisfaction, Depression, and Losses," *European Journal of Work and Organizational Psychology* 26, no. 6 (2017): 811–827.

5. Retirement Confidence Survey, "Expectations About Retirement," 2022 RCS Fact Sheet #2, https://www.ebri.org/docs/default-source/rcs/2022-rcs/rcs_22-fs-2.pdf. Interestingly, although 7 in 10 plan to work, only 27% report actually doing this!

6. T. Olds et al., "One Day You'll Wake Up and Won't Have to Go to Work: The Impact of Changes in Time Use on Mental Health Following Retirement," *PLoS One* 13, no. 6 (2018): p.e.

7. K. Strauss, "Future Work Selves: How Hoped for Identities Motivate Proactive Behaviour at Work," *Semantic Scholar*, 2010, https://www.semanticscholar.org/paper/Future-work-selves-%3A-how-hoped-for-identities-at-Strauss/bc63daadcf76a4b5c25b1e96221b24d4248c52ec?p2df.

CHAPTER 6

Retire with Purpose

by John Coleman

Rufus Massey led a vibrant career. He was born in Chickamauga, Georgia, in a rough-board, two-room cabin his father built by hand. There was no phone service. The closest neighbors were about half a mile away. Life was never easy. But the resilience and perseverance he learned in his youth helped to transform his life. Rufus went on to build a remarkable career in corporate America and higher education. At Bell South, he had a firsthand look at the evolution of technology in telecommunications, and both before and after his corporate career, he did stints at his alma mater, Berry College, supporting students and reimagining the school's innovative work program.

A few years ago, Rufus realized it was time to move on from full-time work. But the pace of his life has barely slowed. He's in a barbershop quartet and enters singing competitions around the country. He loves tennis and pickleball, and he spends lots of time with his friends, kids, and grandkids. He returns to the old cabin he inherited from his parents to work on things and enjoy the peace and quiet of the North Georgia mountains. He's a scuba diver. He keeps in touch with some of the hundreds of students he's mentored over the years, and he's even writing a book about his experiences. Rufus's life has changed but not necessarily slowed. "I like challenges," he tells me. "I have always been an adventure kind of person." And this new phase of life certainly shows it. He's traded a purposeful career for a similarly purposeful—if more varied—retirement.

Purpose and meaning are essential to us at any age. In the *HBR Guide to Crafting Your Purpose*, I explore the idea that purpose is built, not found, that each person has multiple sources of meaning in their lives, and that those sources of meaning shift over time. Perhaps none of those shifts in meaning is as complex to navigate as deciding to end—for good—a life of full-time work.

Planning Your Transition with Purpose

Many of us look forward to and plan for retirement for years. The transition can signal a new and exciting phase of life in which you get to explore your passions after a lifetime of studying, working, raising children, caring for aging parents, and otherwise feeling obligated to others. Buttressed by proper financial planning, it can lead to a new kind of freedom. Yet it can also be fraught with peril. Work is an important source of relationships for many of us, and retirees often struggle with loneliness and isolation. Similarly, employment can be a source of structure, cognitive challenge, and meaningful goals—all things you must have a plan to thoughtfully replace as a retiree. And many people struggle with lack of purpose postretirement. Some studies have even showed that early retirement leads to early mortality—though the causes of such a phenomenon are hotly debated.[1]

Transitions are inevitable, and retirement is one of life's most important. But how can you navigate that transition well, building a life of purpose after closing the curtain on a career? I firmly believe that you don't stumble into purpose—you craft it. And retirement offers a unique and exceptional opportunity to craft a brand-new era of your life.

To do this well, you must first proactively approach the transition—seeing clearly what you are leaving behind and creating a picture of what you will replace it with. Retirement isn't the only transition like this in life. Something similar happens when we graduate from college, get married or divorced, have kids, experience the death of family members or close friends, switch jobs, or approach one of life's many other milestones. But embracing that transition and navigating it well requires a structured approach. There are four basic steps to navigating this transition with a sense of purpose:

1. **Identify what's permanent.** During a period of transition and instability, it's more important than ever to identify sources of permanence that

give your life meaning. No matter who you are, you are more than your job, and there are things that make your life purposeful well beyond your profession that you will want to hold fast to. What are they? For many, these include a spouse, children or grandchildren, close friends, cherished hobbies, and religious beliefs. Identifying those in advance and how to rely on them in this new stage of life can be critical to flourishing.

2. **Learn to let go.** All of us become defined, in some ways, by our job. And this may be particularly true of those of us whose personalities cause them to become deeply invested in whatever we do, even finding it difficult to fully unplug for a long vacation. Letting go permanently can feel like losing a core piece of our identity. But to enter this new phase of life, you have to let go of the old. If you're handing off the reins, do so cleanly and fully. When you are leaving your profession, give yourself real time (at least at first) away from your old life to draw clean boundaries of separation.

3. **Embrace others.** Any period of growth, disruption, and change is easier to navigate when experienced with others. Who is going to work through your transition to retirement with you? A spouse? A few close friends? A child or mentor? Leaning on these people during the transition, trusting them with your thoughts and seeking their reflections, and allowing them to think

through life with you can only make the process feel clearer and more manageable. Let the people you'll lean on know who they are and ask them to be a part of the journey. And given that people and relationships are central to both happiness and purpose, the very act of reaching out to others in this transition can lead to a renewed sense of meaning in those encounters.

4. **Reject stagnation.** Boris Groysberg and Robin Abrahams have written eloquently about how you should never run *from* something (like a job) without running *to* something.[2] And that's true even in retirement. As you exit your career and the purpose it gave you, reject the temptation to simply fall into the next phase without a plan. Instead, embrace the opportunity to prepare for this new time in life and the new sources of purpose it might bring.

That last point may be particularly important in navigating the transition of retirement. People are surrounded by multiple sources of purpose well outside the bounds of their careers, and as you embrace the steps of transitioning to a new and purposeful phase of life, there are at least six timeless areas that will be fruitful for you to explore. Clearly reflecting on these areas may both affirm existing areas of meaning in which you can invest and identify new possibilities for you to investigate. I think of them through the acronym LABORS: love, avocations and self-improvement, beauty, occupation, religious or philosophical tradition, and service to others.

Love

The number one determinant of happiness in your life is the depth and breadth of your positive relationships.[3] One of the key pitfalls of aging is the possibility you may fall inadvertently into loneliness and isolation. Counter this proactively by seeking a broad web of positive relationships. The difficult thing about retirement can be leaving those work relationships behind. On the plus side, however, retiring can create space for new relationships and to deepen the ones you already have.

For many, this will start with family. The opportunity for people to invest in spouses, children, and grandchildren is one of the key reasons even people who love their work leave the full-time world. And making time for family is a cliché for a reason: It's important and a critical part of feeling purposeful.

However, relationships don't have to stop there. Like Rufus Massey, you have the opportunity to invest in and with those you previously worked with, potentially even continuing mentorship relationships you formed during your career. As you take up new activities—whether volunteering, running, or learning a musical instrument— you have the opportunity to build community and forge new bonds. And of course, you may have friends also reaching retirement age with whom you can engage in life's adventures together.

Avocations and Self-Improvement

Leaving a full-time career can create extraordinary time to pursue your passions. It can also create space for you to really take care of yourself—exercising, meditating, eating better, and exploring your intellectual curiosities. These avocations and initiatives for self-improvement are an important source of purpose at any age, but their importance is amplified when you leave a career. The key is to remember the goal of retirement isn't "free time" for its own sake, but to pursue the things you love. And identifying those activities and what you hope to accomplish as you approach retirement can help you avoid feeling unmoored.

Isolate in advance those areas of self-improvement—physical health, mental well-being, intellectual development—you hope to take on with your new free time, and set and commit to goals. Find at least two to three hobbies or passion projects you can invest in in a structured way—registering people to vote, learning watercolor painting, designing jewelry for craft fairs, or raising honeybees. They don't have to keep you as busy as your old job, but they should provide some structure to your days and create a sense of challenge and accomplishment.

Beauty

One of the hardest sources of purpose to mine in the midst of a busy career is beauty. I'm not necessarily talking about makeup or highly attractive people, though that may fit your definition. I mean something that pleases your senses. While sitting at a desk all day or traveling for work, it can be difficult to find moments to encounter beauty and take the time to fully appreciate it. But beauty has been shown to have a strong connection with happiness and can offer us such a remarkable sense of purpose and meaning by inspiring, challenging, and entrancing us.[4] Retirement is an extraordinary time enjoy it.

What types of beauty do you love? How can you best experience it? See nature through a cross-country road trip or long hikes in the woods. Visit museums or, perhaps, take up painting. Read those great, leisurely books you've been meaning to read. And take the pottery class you've always had your eye on. Beauty is central to a flourishing life at any age, and the freedom and flexibility of retirement may offer more opportunities to experience beauty than any other time in life.

Occupation

Obviously, the whole point of retirement is leaving full-time work. However, I think each retiree should honestly ask themselves whether retirement means fully abandoning work, or whether it should more rightly be a transition to a phase when work is simply not at the center of life. In this way, I've seen many retirees successfully achieve all the flexibility of retirement while retaining the meaning offered by work through part-time pursuits.

Are there things you would do part-time that might offer you some of the benefits of your prior career— professional challenge, relationships, and intellectual pursuits? Perhaps you've been meaning to write a book. Maybe you can translate your lifetime of experience into teaching a class at a local college. Or you could develop a gig buying and running rental properties or driving for a ride-sharing service to meet interesting people around town. Retirement from full-time work doesn't have to mean fully abandoning work—it can be as simple as reshaping it to better fit a new and more relaxed phase of life.

Religious or Philosophical Tradition

For most people, aging is a time of reflection. You have accumulated a lifetime of experiences and wisdom, and you are closer to your own mortality than ever before. Even for those who have not been very religious or philosophical to date, retirement can provide an excellent opportunity to ask thoughtful questions about the nature of life.

Around 85% of the world's population identifies with a religion, and even more have some sort of moral and philosophical tradition to which they adhere.[5] A number of studies have shown that religious believers tend to be happier and more civically engaged and even experience better health outcomes, particularly when they are engaged in community or in contemplative practices like prayer.[6] And ancient and modern wisdom reminds us "the unexamined life is not worth living." In the frenetic cadence of a workweek, it's easy to get busy and push the big questions about existence to the side. But retirement can provide space to ask these questions and garner meaning from the answers you find.

If you already have some sort of religious or philosophical belief, take the opportunity to invest in it more deeply. Volunteer at your church, synagogue, or other place of worship or read books about your belief system with others. If you are searching or uncertain, take the time for exploration. Very few people regret investigating life's deeper meaning, and for many it provides a remarkable source of centering and fulfillment.

Service to Others

Nothing has the ability to immediately transform a life quite like service to others. Various studies have indicated that service to others is at the heart of creating meaning and purpose in one's life.[7] Research has also found that volunteering counters stress, combats depression, creates happiness, increases self-confidence, and even positively correlates with physical health.[8] And we all know that when we serve others, we feel happier and more fulfilled, motivated, and engaged.

Who can you serve in retirement? Perhaps you can read in a local school or be a mentor through a program in your community. You could work in a homeless shelter or volunteer to clean up a park. You could spend more time helping out around your local mosque or serve on the board of the local children's hospital or ballet company. Finding ways to serve others with your new free time and with the experiences you've accumulated can ensure retirement isn't a totally self-centered or meaningless pursuit.

Preparing to thoughtfully navigate your retirement transition by cultivating new sources of purpose through relationships, service to others, admiring beauty, embracing life's big questions, and finding constructive hobbies or part-time work to occupy your talents can mean the difference between a rudderless retirement and one filled with a new and exciting purpose.

———————

John Coleman is the author of the *HBR Guide to Crafting Your Purpose*. Subscribe to his free newsletter, *On Purpose*, or contact him at johnwilliamcoleman.com.

NOTES

1. Nicole Torres, "You're Likely to Live Longer If You Retire After 65," *Harvard Business Review*, June 2016, 28–29.

2. Boris Groysberg and Robin Abrahams, "Managing Yourself: Five Ways to Bungle a Job Change," *Harvard Business Review*, January–February 2010, 137–140.

3. Greg Bell, "The Decades-Long Grant Study's Conclusion: 'Happiness Is Love. Full Stop,'" *Deseret News*, March 6, 2015.

4. Cody C. Delistraty, "The Beauty-Happiness Connection," *Atlantic*, August 15, 2014.

5. World Population Review, "Religion by Country 2022," https://worldpopulationreview.com/country-rankings/religion-by-country.

6. "Religion's Relationship to Happiness, Civic Engagement and Health Around the World," Pew Research Center, January 31, 2019, https://www.pewresearch.org/religion/2019/01/31/religions-relationship-to-happiness-civic-engagement-and-health-around-the-world; Nicole Rura, "Spirituality Linked with Better Health Outcomes, Patient Care," *Harvard Gazette*, July 12, 2022; Kristen Rogers, "The Psychological Benefits of Prayer: What Science Says About the Mind-Soul Connection," CNN, June 17, 2020, https://www.cnn.com/2020/06/17/health/benefits-of-prayer-wellness/index.html.

7. Gleb Tsipursky, "Is Serving Others the Key to Meaning and Purpose?," *Psychology Today*, July 14, 2016.

8. Trish Lockard, "How Volunteering Improves Mental Health," NAMI, February 2, 2022; Stephanie Watson, "Volunteering May Be Good for Body and Mind," Harvard Health Publishing, June 26, 2013.

CHAPTER 7

Learn to Get Better at Transitions

by Avivah Wittenberg-Cox

There is a small, disheveled baby robin making her very first steps in my garden today. She looks a bit dazed and exhausted, her lovely yellow down all awry. I know exactly what she feels like. She looks like a lot of people I know right now. At almost every age, everyone seems to be on the cusp of a similar transition: taking their first steps into an uncertain and illegible new world.

At just shy of 57, I feel poised between two ends of the spectrum, baby bird and great-grandmother. From this middle spot, I can observe my entire family hanging, in a seemingly collective cliff ritual, on the edge of

Adapted from content posted on hbr.org, July 5, 2018 (product #H04FD4).

change. We are all transitioning—quasi-simultaneously and quite unexpectedly—into our next chapters. My daughter is graduating from college. My son is starting his first company. My husband is adapting to something he resists calling retirement. My mother has just been fitted with her first hearing aids and is suddenly complaining about the noise of the sirens in the city. Not to mention my trio of good friends, one who lost a job, one who moved to another country, and one who split from her partner.

Every one of this cross-generational crew is struggling to let go of *what was* (identity, community, colleagues, and competencies) to embrace what's next (as yet unknown, undefined, and ambiguous). There is a mixture of fear (*Who am I?*) and excitement (*I am SO ready for a change*), confusion (*What do I want?*) and certainty (*Time to move on*).

Because more of us are living longer, healthier lives, we'll face more of these moments of liminality. And so I'm sitting in the garden, watching Robin Jr. test her fledgling wings, researching how to prepare for the several decades still ahead. No matter where we are in our own journeys, we could all get better at the skill of transitioning. To do this, focus on five component skills.

Pacing and planning

Longevity means that, more than ever, we need to plan for change. Using the gift of decades requires acknowledging their existence and deciding what you want to do with them. People say you can't have it all, but the gift of time gives us new options to have a lot more than we ever thought possible.

- Measure out your life to date in major chapters. Erik Erikson mapped out adulthood in seven-year periods. What were the highlights, accomplishments, and learnings of each of your past seven-year periods?

- How many seven-year periods do you have before you hit 100?

- Draw a timeline from 0 to 100 and place yourself on it. This gives you an idea of the possible length of the road ahead.

Leaving gracefully

There comes a time in jobs, life phases, or relationships where you know an arc has reached its end. Knowing when it is time to end—and ending well—will become an increasingly valuable skill as lives lengthen and transitions become multiple across both personal and professional lives. Ends can come from within, the result of burnout or boredom, depression or exhaustion. Or they can come from without, the land of restructurings and layoffs, divorce or other major life shifts. They are the prequel to re-creation. It is not always an easy time —for anyone involved, at work or at home. We can spend quite a lot of it loitering unproductively, wondering whether we should stay or go. But good endings are the best building blocks to good beginnings.

- Choosing to choose gives you agency. The choice itself, sometimes made years before you actually move, is the first, and often the biggest, step.

- Ask yourself if you are staying where you are out of love, or out of fear. Do you love where you are, or do you fear leaving it for a murky unknown? The latter is a lousy place from which to live, but many of us stay stuck here. *Who would I be without this title, this salary, or this position?* It can be an exciting question, not a scary one.

- Embrace confusion, ambiguity, and questions. There redefinition lies. And remember, you don't have to face them alone.

Letting the inside out

Self-knowledge is one of the hard-won rewards of aging. For many of us, our inner selves remain unexplored territory until the second half of adulthood. My friend Mary had yearned for creative outlets much of her life but had never considered herself artistic until she took up writing and painting in her sixties. At 80, she is a successful artist and published poet. What part of yourself might be waiting, hidden in the wings? A few questions to set you on your way:

- What have you most enjoyed in your career to date?

- What kinds of people energize you, and what kinds of environments shut you down?

- Do you want to transfer skills or start from scratch and reinvent? Build on accomplishments or never hear of them again?

- What kind of balance will you prioritize for this phase? Focus on one thing or cumulate a series of side hustles into a portfolio life?

- Do you want to anchor security or toss it to the winds?

In this journey, which can take a few years, you'll want to pack a comforting "travel bag": an advisory board of trusted supporters, a realistic timeline, a financial plan, and clearly negotiated support from your partner, if you have one. Preparing for the next third of your life requires more than updating your LinkedIn profile. Invest in the next phase as you would in any seven-year project. Seriously.

Letting the outside in

Any transition plan will benefit from feedback from the outside world. Essentially, you're market testing your new plan, and figuring out where you're most needed and appreciated. Clare and Mark thought that when they reached their early sixties, they'd retire and leave their U.K. base to live in a new country. So, in their fifties, they took a sabbatical from work and lived in four different countries for three months each to find the perfect place. In the end, this experience helped them decide to enter a new profession instead of a new country. They decided to move to a new home just an hour from where they'd been living and start an eco-friendly farm, fulfilling a long-held passion for sustainability and food.

This is a process London Business School professor Herminia Ibarra calls "outsight"—actually visiting these metaphorical new lands to discover not only what you love but where you are loved. Her point is that insight alone may not be enough:

- What do others most appreciate about you?

- What have you done or worked on that elicits the best response, the most appreciation, or follow-up?

- Which of your experiments have attracted the kind of questions, people, or projects that excite you?

- When, where, and with whom did you feel most alive?

Leaping

Seeing people who have transitioned successfully to a new phase and invested in something they deeply care about, sometimes for the first time in their lives, is an inspiring sight. Some people only really find, or allow themselves to find, their calling after they've fulfilled all their duties—to their own earlier expectations, to parents, to family. The freedom that comes from finally aligning with yourself is profound. Neither fame nor fortune can feed the unsatisfied soul. As Erich Fromm wrote half a century ago, "The whole life of the individual is nothing but the process of giving birth to himself; indeed, we should be fully born when we die—although it is the tragic fate of most individuals to die before they are born."

Now that we have a few extra decades to test our wings, the real challenge may be remembering that it's never too late to fly.

––––––––––

Avivah Wittenberg-Cox is CEO of 20-first, a gender and generational consulting firm; a Harvard Advanced Leadership Initiative (ALI) Fellow '22; and the author of *Seven Steps to Leading a Gender-Balanced Business* (Harvard Business Review Press, 2014).

Consider Your Options—and Ways Forward

CHAPTER 8

Plan a Satisfying Retirement

by Rebecca Knight

You've worked hard all your life, and now you're on the brink of retirement. Trouble is, the things you looked forward to all those years—leisurely mornings, afternoons puttering in the garden, trips to exotic places—don't feel like they'll be enough to sustain you. Encore careers—jobs that blend income, personal meaning, and often some element of giving back—are becoming an increasingly popular alternative to full-time retirement. But where do you start?

Adapted from content posted on hbr.org, September 4, 2014 (product #H00Z08).

What the Experts Say

According to Encore.org, a think tank focused on baby boomers, work, and social purpose, nearly 9 million people ages 44 to 70 today are engaged in second-act careers. "People are leading longer and healthier lives and so leaving full-time work in your mid-60s means that you're looking at a horizon of 20 to 30 years. That's a long time," says Marc Freedman, CEO of Encore.org and the author of *The Big Shift*. There is, he says, the financial question of how you'll support yourself, "and then there is the existential question: Who you are going to be?"

On one hand, it's daunting to contemplate embarking on a new career at this stage in life. On the other hand, it's liberating to let go of the past and forge a new identity based on "things that you find exciting, stimulating, or interesting," says Ron Ashkenas, a senior partner at Schaffer Consulting and an executive-in-residence at UC Berkeley's Haas School of Business. "It's an opportunity to think about how you want to contribute to society, your community, and your family." Karen Dillon, coauthor of *How Will You Measure Your Life?*, agrees: "Life doesn't necessarily get simpler after you leave a full-time job," she says. "But it can become more rewarding—if you're willing to hold yourself accountable and work for the new goals you've set yourself." Here are some things to think about as you prepare for this new phase.

Lay the groundwork early

If you're confident that your job won't be in jeopardy, tell colleagues about your plans to officially retire while you're still gainfully employed. "Then it's not out of the blue, and it also gives them a chance to figure out if they have contacts or a network you could leverage," says Ashkenas. It's also important that you leave on good terms with your company and indicate if you are open to occasional projects and assignments—which is a good way to keep your hand in your profession. Adds Dillon: "You can't just stop working and expect the phone to ring. Plant seeds early so that once you're in circulation, experiences and opportunities will come to you."

Don't rush

Once you leave your job, give yourself a period of time— ideally months in duration—to reflect on what you want to do next. "Give yourself time to rest, renew, and re-store," says Freedman. Navigating this transition will take some time. "You've been working and juggling family stuff for decades and likely haven't had the time to think about this next chapter of your life. Recognize that finding work that is significant and fulfilling could take two to three years."

Ask yourself: What's really important?

Make a list of all the things that feed you emotionally and then drill down to figure out exactly what it is about those things that inspires you and makes you happy, suggests Dillon. For instance, you might list spending time with your kids or doing work that's challenging, but "what you most enjoy is having new experiences with your children, like travel. And what you really like about work is collaborating with others and creating something," says Dillon. "Push yourself to do the things that matter to you and be conscious of the choices you're making and how you're spending your time." Your goal, says Freedman, is to "figure out what your priorities are at this juncture in your life."

Be willing to experiment

Freedman advises taking a "try-before-you-buy" approach. "Find ways to dabble in things that interest you," he says. Seek out internships, fellowships, or part-time jobs; give back by volunteering to serve on a board of a nonprofit; take on different kinds of professional assignments; or sign up for a class at a community college. "If it sounds fun and interesting and it seems as though you will learn new things, do it," says Dillon. Also look for ways to transfer your hard-earned expertise to new domains, says Ashkenas. "It's not as if you stop being who you are. You are still you, and you still have the same skills; you're just applying them to new situations and environments."

Keep productive

After you've given yourself some time off, it's important to return to some of the things that office life gave you: structure and community. "Just as you would look ahead to milestones in your work, you need things to look forward to and anticipate," Ashkenas says. Consider joining a group or community like an alumni association, a volunteer or religious organization, a freelancers' group, a book club, or even a virtual community. After all, "you need the stuff you get from the informal office environment: banter, chatter, laughter, and information," Dillon adds. It's also helpful to spend time with others who are "wrestling with the same challenges you are," says Freedman.

Hold yourself accountable

As you're navigating this transition, "you have to think about goals," says Dillon. "Get feedback from those you care about—like your spouse or partner, children, and friends—about how you're doing. And be honest with yourself about how you're spending your time. Do a reality check by asking yourself, 'Do I feel good and healthy? Do I feel stimulated?' Don't let outside voices dictate your answers," says Dillon. And once you figure out where you want to focus, Ashkenas says, "you need to keep asking yourself: 'Am I adding value? Am I making a contribution? Am I learning something?'"

Case Study: Leverage Your Expertise and Connections to Give Back

Bill Haggett spent the first part of his career in the shipbuilding business—first as president and CEO of Bath Iron Works in Maine and later as the head of Irving Shipbuilding of New Brunswick, Canada. After leaving Irving in the late 1990s and returning to Maine, Bill wanted to give back to his community.

His first priority: building a new YMCA in his hometown. Bill helped raise funds for the Y and also helped design the new complex. "I grew up in Bath, Maine, in the 1940s and I am from a family of modest means," he says. "The YMCA was a terrific outlet for me and my friends."

By 2000, the Y project was complete, but Bill wasn't interested in "moving into retirement mode." The Libra Foundation, a large charitable organization in Maine, approached him about a job. "They wanted to make a strategic investment in a potato company in northern Maine on the brink of bankruptcy. And they asked: 'Would I be willing to serve as chairman and CEO?'"

Bill knew nothing about the potato business, and he had little interest in moving to northern Maine. But after reflecting on what he wanted out of the next chapter of his life, he realized the opportunity was appealing. "It was a way to help the economy by adding value and jobs in that part of the state," he says. The job would be fulfilling on a personal level too. "I wanted the challenge of turning this business around. It was a way to learn something new, but I also thought I had some expertise I could bring to the party."

The early years were a struggle, but after a while, business at Naturally Potatoes improved: Sales increased by 40%, and the company returned to profitability. By 2005, it was sold to California-based Basic America Foods (BAF). Bill, meanwhile, went on to run a meat company. But Naturally Potatoes fell short of BAF's expectations, and when, in 2010, a team led by Libra bought the company back, Bill resumed the role of CEO.

At the age of 80, Bill—who is chairman and CEO of Pineland Farms Natural Meats *and* Pineland Farms Potatoes—has no plans to stop working. "I feel energized," he says. "One of the great pleasures of being my age is that everyone I work with is younger than I am. They have bright ideas, skills, and technology savvy that

I don't have." Learning a new business every few years has been "stimulating," he says. "I like to be useful and to make a contribution."

Rebecca Knight is currently a senior correspondent at *Insider* covering careers and the workplace. Previously she was a freelance journalist and a lecturer at Wesleyan University. Her work has been published in the *New York Times*, *USA Today*, and the *Financial Times*.

CHAPTER 9

How to Figure Out What You Want to Do When You "Grow Up"

by Gorick Ng

On the eve of her retirement, I asked school superintendent Sue Pfeffer, "What's next?"

"I don't know!" she replied. "I'm still figuring out what I want to do when I 'grow up.'"

I froze. I didn't know how to respond.

"Life is a journey," she clarified, smiling. "That's what makes it fun. I'm still growing. I'm still learning. I'll stop when I'm dead."

Journey? I repeated to myself. *Fun?*

I was skeptical.

After all, just earlier, I had met an investment banker who, after making it to the top, started wondering if she was meant to be a banker. "I went into finance because that's what you did with a business degree from my school," she admitted. "But was that what I really wanted? I had no idea."

I met a software engineer at a technology company who, after shutting down his startup and taking "a real job," started second-guessing himself. "I'm so happy here," he told me. "I love the stability. But somehow everyone's making me question if I *should* be happy."

I met another individual—a current college student—who had just returned from their school's career fair, only to end up more confused. "My mentors keep telling me that I can do whatever I want," they sighed. "But what if I'm passionate about everything and nothing at the same time?"

Despite the different career stages and contexts, these individuals had something in common: They were all wrestling with what they want versus what they *want* to want, with what they *could* be doing versus *should be* doing, and with who they *were* versus who they *are*.

And after conducting over 500 interviews with professionals at all career stages to write my *Wall Street Journal* bestselling book, *The Unspoken Rules*, I am convinced they're not alone. Whether you're just starting your career or winding down like Sue, grappling with large questions like these doesn't end—nor should it.

How do we find clarity in the face of ambiguity? By seeing our careers as Sue did: as a lifelong journey. Your journey begins with your first job and extends through midcareer (and possible new careers), to retirement (whatever that may be and whether or not it exists), and beyond. And like any journey, a successful one requires thoughtful reflection, planning, packing, and steering. You don't and can't know all that lies ahead, but these practices can help you manage the forks in the road that can appear at any stage of your career.

Step 1: Reflect Regularly

Imagine you're taking a road trip. Your first task isn't to start driving—it's to decide what type of trip you're taking. Some people have a certain destination in mind and want to get there as quickly as possible. Others don't care if they miss a highway exit or two. They're in a hurry for the photos, friends, and stories.

Asking yourself, "What matters more: the journey or the destination?" isn't just a road-trip question; it's also a career and life question.

When you think about your current career journey—or the path you'd like to explore next—are you striving to reach a certain role (for example, CEO), contribute to a certain cause (for example, climate change), help a certain group (for example, refugees), attain a certain lifestyle (for example, vacation around the world, own a certain type of car), or retire by a certain age? If so, you might be one of the more destination-focused drivers on the road.

Conversely, do you prioritize work-life balance, doing purposeful work, developing your knowledge and skills, working with people you like, or being financially stable? If so, you might be a more journey-focused driver—and might want to keep one eye on the road and the other on the passing scenery.

Just because you aspire to become a corporate law firm partner doesn't mean you're evil. Just because you *don't* aspire to become one doesn't mean you're lazy. Just because you *were* a corporate law firm partner and *no longer* want to be one doesn't mean you're indecisive. Your goals don't have to be the same as everyone else's. Your goals also don't have to stay the same. In fact, they probably shouldn't, especially as you enter and leave different chapters of life. What's most important is that you know why you're doing what you're doing at this moment in time. And if you're nearing the end of a particular journey, remember that every journey ends the same way: in anticipation of the next adventure. So, keep reflecting. As Sue taught me, it's never too late.

Step 2: Plan Deliberately

Open your maps app, drop a pin, and you'll find multiple possible routes and estimated times of arrival. Your job is to decide which path you'd like to start with, even if you decide to make up your own route later.

Planning your career—and what comes after your formal career ends—is no different. Open any individual's Wikipedia page, biography, or LinkedIn profile and you'll find a rough timeline of what they did to get where they are today. Though no profile is complete and every profile has its embellishments, this research can help you uncover the patterns inherent to each career path, the choices and sacrifices that await you, and where you might want to follow others' footsteps or pave your own way forward.

You'll notice from Wikipedia, for example, that many Hollywood actors spent years modeling or appearing in commercials before being cast in a major feature film. On LinkedIn, you'll see that many private equity investors didn't start their careers in private equity, but in investment banking. You'll learn from podcasts and blogs that many entrepreneurs didn't quit their jobs impulsively; many experimented with side projects until they demonstrated enough demand and built enough confidence to pursue their ventures full-time. Everyone starts somewhere and ends up somewhere—and every profession has patterns. This research has an added benefit: You'll discover how others approached a career pause or retirement, whether by returning to school, joining a board, volunteering, starting a business, moving abroad, or any other option.

Once you've identified a few paths that intrigue you, the next step is to ask for help. Contact a few people who've taken a similar path, request a call, and ask them questions such as "I noticed you went from X to Y. How did you make the transition?" You could also ask, "Given X and Y, what's your advice on what I should do next?" Every person will have biases, but travel guides can only get you so far. Nothing beats asking a local for recommendations.

While you're learning and contemplating new routes, don't forget to ask yourself: "Whose path most intrigues me?" So, as you're analyzing the people who've come before you, make two lists: *personal* role models and *professional* role models. On the personal front, consider whose life you would most like to *live* and whose values would you most like to *live by*. On the professional side, consider whose work and contributions inspire you most. No one is perfect. Having multiple role models helps account for life's complexities.

Step 3: Pack Strategically

Different terrain requires different shoes and tires. Different countries require different entry visas. But no matter where you go, you will never regret packing a toothbrush and enough pairs of underwear.

The same logic applies to navigating each stage of your career journey: Different career paths will give you credit for different credentials, but all career paths will value the same credentials. No matter which path you choose or the road or weather conditions you encounter, you can expect to pack the same no-regret items: the ability to speak and write well, build relationships, and learn quickly—the skills that are also unlikely to get automated. So, get comfortable writing, speaking, and meeting people. While you're at it, get into the habit of staying on top of the news, especially the domains you're intrigued by. You'll be able to not only communicate with more people if you know what's happening and what's hot in their world, but also know which opportunities to pursue.

Regardless of the path you pursue, the more senior you are in an organization, the more you become a salesperson—for your team, your ideas, and yourself. If you start your career as a software engineer, for example, the verb you can expect to repeat daily is "coding." By the time you reach vice president of engineering, however, your daily verb is no longer coding—it's "selling": You're selling ideas to the higher-ups to garner resources, selling ideas to your team to build enthusiasm, and selling ideas to outsiders to attract talent—not to mention business. So, to the extent your journey involves getting promoted, be prepared to continue upgrading and replenishing your "pack," especially with the skill of selling.

On top of the no-regret packing list, every path also expects you to have additional supplies. Interested in data science? Keep up with the latest analytical methods. Pursuing a career in marketing? Stay up to date on the latest trends, terms, and tools. No one will explicitly tell you to develop these skills and keep them sharp over the long haul, but those who stay ahead—or stay relevant— will. So, whether you sign on to stretch assignments at work, take on a side project, or return to school, you need to unpack and repack as your journey continues.

Step 4: Steer Flexibly

Whether it's a flat tire, a road closure, a sudden craving, a health issue, or all of the above, knowing when and how to switch lanes—or maybe even get off the highway altogether—is crucial to your overall journey.

In navigating your career journey for the long haul, steering around changing industries and changing jobs—not to mention your own evolving interests and values over the course of your career—can mean the difference between staying fulfilled and feeling stuck and not knowing why. After all, your job in 10 years may not even exist yet—just as the job you *think* you might want in 10 years may not exist then. Similarly, the job you think you want in 10 years may not be the job you want then. To make the journey even more complex, different paths may put different emphasis on different skills, knowledge, networks, and credentials. (Just ask the academics who have to truncate their 20-page scholarly publication–filled CVs down to a one-page résumé for industry jobs; it's not easy switching lanes.)

The key is to be aware of the patterns of the road—and to flexibly steer around them.

One key pattern to overcome is the age-old chicken-and-egg problem where you need relevant experience to get relevant experience—and few people are willing to give a chance to someone who's unproven, no matter your age or career stage. For those early in their careers, such a chicken-and-egg problem often means convincing an employer to give you a chance at that marketing role, even if you've only ever worked in retail. For those later in their careers, it often means being labeled overqualified, too expensive, or not having the right background despite your decades of experience. In general, switching industries and functions (for example, from sales at a pharmaceutical company to human resources at an insurance company) will be the most challenging because your background looks so foreign to your new employer. Switching neither industry nor function (for example, from pharmaceutical sales at one company to pharmaceutical sales at another) will be easier. Changing one variable—either industry or function—is still challenging, but doable. So, be mindful of which variable you're changing. Bootcamps, graduate school, or "returnships" (programs for those who took a career break) may help, but how well you transition will more often depend on how well you plan. When in doubt, exercise your professional online search skills by analyzing what alums of your desired program do after graduation. If they are doing what you plan to do, you're on the right track. If not, consider looking more broadly.

Another key pattern is the age-old adage, "You have to see it to believe it." It's true: The best way to figure out if you'll like a certain ice cream flavor isn't to spend more time reviewing the options—it's to give it a try. If you've started down a path and are deciding whether to continue or if you haven't yet started and are frozen with analysis paralysis, give it a try. Just as our map apps aren't great at figuring out if we're facing north or south until we start walking, the key to finding your direction isn't to stand still; it's to move in any direction. So, move—and start collecting more information: Ask for an introduction to someone you're intrigued by; volunteer for projects beyond your daily task list; and yes, consider picking up a side project. At worst, you'll learn what you don't like; at best, you might uncover a different path that either fits your journey or helps you get closer to your goal.

Richard Zhang, a PhD turned real estate investor, once told me about the three phases of his career journey: Phase one involved living up to his parents' definition of success—so he worked hard in school, got a good GPA, and pursued a graduate degree in a field he didn't see as a career. Phase two involved living up to society's definition of success—so he left the world of academia, pursued a corporate job in a field unrelated to his studies but that all his friends had vied for, and worked himself into the ground. Phase three involved living up to his own definition of success—which included leaving his corporate job, exercising, eating a healthy diet, and working in a field that excited him.

As I reflected on the investment banker searching for meaning, the software engineer seeking satisfaction, and the college student looking for direction—not to mention Sue, who was anticipating what's next—I noticed that we are all on a journey toward living up to our own definitions of success. We don't always know the path our careers will take; we don't always control when parts of our journey end. But at any stage of our careers, reflecting, planning, packing, and steering will help you enjoy the ride, no matter its length or where it takes you.

Gorick Ng is the *Wall Street Journal* bestselling author of *The Unspoken Rules: Secrets to Starting Your Career Off Right* (Harvard Business Review Press, 2021). He is a career adviser at Harvard, specializing in coaching first-generation college students and professionals. He also teaches the unspoken rules of career navigation at UC Berkeley. He has been featured in the *New York Times*, CNBC, the *Today Show*, and more, and was named one of the top 30 thinkers to watch by Thinkers50. Find him at www.gorick.com.

CHAPTER 10

Reeling from a Sudden Job Loss? Here's How to Start Healing

by Silviana Falcon and Kandi Wiens

Mike had been a successful executive for more than 20 years, turning troubled departments into efficient and quality-driven business lines. When a new leadership team took over the organization, he witnessed a shift in vision and an abundance of deceit, distrust, and betrayal. Mike spoke out against cost-cutting initiatives that compromised safety and quality standards until he was told his services were no longer needed.

Adapted from content posted on hbr.org, July 5, 2022 (product #H074EO).

Unfortunately, Mike's experience is far from unique. Sudden job loss can occur when you're terminated or laid off, when you resign because you feel you have no choice (for example, you observe ethical violations in your organization that you don't want to be a part of), when you're moved to a different role within your organization, when your company taps you for a forced early retirement, or when you're burned out and choose to leave.

Regardless of the reason, the sudden loss of a job can be nothing short of traumatic. Mike worked hard to be successful, and he'd devoted decades of his career to this organization. His grief was gut-wrenching, leaving him to deal with feelings of anger, betrayal, isolation, shame, and hopelessness.

Those emotions can feel intense, unwieldy, and even unmanageable, especially when you've attained a certain position or income level, when you bear the financial responsibility of a household, when work has become an intrinsic marker of your moral worth, or when you feel like you've reached an age or career stage when starting over feels impossible or unpleasant. You may also notice that the forced transition disrupts your routines, triggers unhealthy coping habits, and places significant strain on relationships with your family, friends, and partner if you have one.

Amid the anguish, it's critical that you reach out for help so that you can regain your mental clarity and ability to take healthy, productive next steps. Consider these tips to help you stay whole through this process, reconnect to your purpose, and most importantly, heal.

Practice self-compassion

You may feel a sense of shame or guilt if you focus on taking care of yourself after a sudden job loss. You may be beating yourself up and wondering, *What did I do to deserve this? What could I have done to prevent it?* But now is the time, like no other, to practice self-compassion.

First, recognize that this is one of the toughest times in your life, so you need to be extra gentle on yourself. Then, double down on reconnecting with people you love outside of work—spend quality time with them to brighten your mood, alleviate tension, and contribute to your sense of connection to others. Allow yourself to be vulnerable by courageously sharing your feelings with others and accepting their help and support.

Attend to your unmet needs

Using neuroscientist David Rock's SCARF model as a framework, losing a job—regardless of the reason—violates all five human social dimensions: our sense of **st**atus (our relative importance to others), **c**ertainty (ability to predict the future), **a**utonomy (feeling of control over events), **r**elatedness (safety with others), and **f**airness (justice).[1]

For many people, losing a job is one of the most stressful and painful events they've experienced. If this sounds like you, don't minimize how you feel. Give yourself permission to grieve, as well as enough time to think about what you need to heal. Focus on making yourself whole again in body and mind.

Start by keeping a journal outlining what you feel you've lost and what you need to move forward. Then, add a list of people and experiences you're thankful for or are looking forward to. This will help you shift your mental focus from loss and uncertainty to control and forward momentum.

Focus on what you can control

Use your emotional intelligence to regulate an over- or underreaction to your present conditions and to focus on what you can control. Seeking an explanation for why it happened to you is counterproductive, because it keeps you anchored in the past and undermines forward momentum.

Acknowledge your brutal reality while maintaining a level of optimism and an understanding that, eventually, you will make it through. This puts you in a problem-solving mode as opposed to an emotional self-control mode. This is key to letting go and moving on.

Take small steps at first by doing something that uses your skills and abilities, like volunteering for an organization you care about. It will help you regain your confidence, contribute to your sense of meaningful work, and reduce your stress level.

Accept what you can't control and prepare to move on

Even though you didn't ask for it, try to embrace this change and learn from it. Don't become your own obstacle by instinctively resisting new possibilities or opportunities. Instead, take this opportunity to self-reflect on the positive lessons you learned from the job you just lost.

This will prove invaluable during your next job interviews, should you decide to move forward in that way. It's a challenge to put on a happy face for a recruiter or hiring manager while you're grieving your old job and fearing rejection once again. While you cannot control the outcome of an interview, you can use the lessons from your last job as a motivator to develop strong answers for your next interview. This will improve your self-confidence, which will be reflected in your body language.

Shift your perspective and stay open-minded

Focusing on the possibilities of the future and a vision of your ideal self will gradually shift your emotional response from grief and loss to feelings of composure, control, and confidence. Recognize that shifting from shock and grief to the hope of new possibilities takes time, effort, and intention. Use the forced transition as a gift.

Am I retired now or back on the job market?

If a corporate restructure unexpectedly accelerates your retirement plans, you may find yourself evaluating whether you're out of a job or out of the job market for good. And you're probably wrestling with some pretty big questions, like: "Am I retired now? Do I try to get a new job? If not, what lies ahead?"

As you contemplate whether you stay retired or explore other job opportunities, consider these questions to help you decide:

- What do you want your days to look like, and how do you see work fitting into your life?

- What do you need financially in order to support your desired lifestyle?

- Who do you want to serve or support with your skills and talents? How?

- What do you want to learn in this next phase of your life?

- What do you want and need in life and/or from work in order to feel your best?

As you move forward and begin to explore what's next, stay open to taking an "in-between" job—perhaps with a decrease in pay if you can swing it, or one that's not in your desired field—and treat it as an opportunity for growth rather than seeing it as a setback or a failure. While sudden job loss marks an undeniably painful and stressful season in your career, you can use the time to reset, recenter, and redefine how you want to live your life so that whatever you decide to do next ultimately reflects who you are, and not the other way around.

It's easy to forget that you're filling a role in an organization and that your job doesn't define you. This is especially true when you're always on and never quite leave work. When you can separate your work from your purpose, you'll find that a job is just a job, and that your purpose lives in you, and just like you, it adapts, changes, and matures over time. As economist Umair Haque has written: "Purpose is a process, not a state; an ever-unfinished accomplishment, not an algorithm." Take time to consider not just what you want to do next, but also who you want to serve with your work.

Mike used the time after his sudden job loss to reevaluate what he really stood for in life, who he wanted to serve, and how he saw his career aligning with his purpose. He'd long dreamed of teaching and found an adjunct position with a local university. It came with a decrease in salary, but an undeniable increase in his sense of wholeness. A year later, when a full-time position became available, Mike went for it. Three years after that, he was named professor of the year.

———————

Silviana Falcon is an assistant professor and the Tanner Endowed Chair of Business Ethics and Economics at the Barney Barnett School of Business and Free Enterprise at Florida Southern College. She is the author of *Lectures and Play: A Practical and Fun Guide to Create Extraordinary Higher Education Classroom Experiences*. **Kandi Wiens** is a senior fellow at the University of Pennsylvania Graduate School of Education, where she is codirector of the Penn Master's in Medical Education Program and the Penn Health Professions Education Certificate Program. She has extensive teaching experience in various Wharton executive education programs and in the PennCLO Executive Doctoral Program and is an executive coach and national speaker. Her forthcoming book, *Burnout Immunity*, will be published in 2024.

NOTE

1. David Rock is the cofounder and CEO of the NeuroLeadership Institute; "5 Ways to Spark (or Destroy) Your Employees' Motivation," NeuroLeadership Institute, September 13, 2022, https://neuroleadership.com/your-brain-at-work/scarf-model-motivate-your-employees.

CHAPTER 11

How to Become a Coach or Consultant After You Retire

by Dorie Clark

The vast majority of senior professionals don't want to retire. They have interesting, fulfilling work that they'd like to continue—just not at the frenetic pace of top corporate jobs. That's why so many, lured by the promise of flexible hours, higher rates, and location independence, are intrigued by the idea of becoming a consultant or coach when they retire from their "official" career. Of

---

Adapted from content posted on hbr.org, May 12, 2017 (product #H03NN7).

course, competition for these plum positions is growing. A 2020 study estimated that there are more than 71,000 professional coaches worldwide, and the British paper the *Independent* pegged the number of management consultants at 500,000.[1]

Given that the majority of coaches in North America are baby boomers, how can you differentiate yourself in a crowded field filled with your high-level peers? Here are five things to keep in mind if you'd like to become a consultant or coach after you retire.

Give Yourself Sufficient Runway

Any career change is disruptive to a certain extent. The more time you give yourself to plan and prepare, the better off you'll be (one to two years is good, and three to four years is better). Albert DiBernardo, who is now the head of strategy and development for a major engineering firm, gave his board three years' notice, and in his performance review, he set a specific retirement date. "My 'new beginning' was cast in that moment," he said, "and it felt great."

Though some people might be concerned about acquiring lame-duck status, giving your company plenty of time for succession planning allows you to make a thoughtful departure and cap your career knowing your legacy is in good hands. Even if you prefer not to tell colleagues about your intentions so far in advance, creating your own internal timetable can allow you to plan your finances and any life changes (moving, selling your house, etc.) that your retirement and new career might entail.

Do a Skills Analysis

Over the years you've probably become an expert in your field. But becoming an independent coach or consultant requires a suite of entrepreneurial abilities on top of your subject-matter knowledge. If you've given yourself a sufficient planning horizon, you can take the opportunity to bolster necessary skills, such as public speaking and social media.

You might also consider pursuing a certification—though debates rage about whether these are worthwhile—or taking targeted courses to accelerate your knowledge.[2] They could be executive education courses offered by universities or programs offered directly by professionals about everything from creating online courses to becoming a recognized expert.[3]

Start Recruiting Clients

Too many aspiring coaches and consultants waste time at the outset dithering about the administrative details of their business, like what color their logo should be. All of that is a moot point until you have actual clients, so recruiting them should be your first priority. To gain experience as a coach or consultant, take on a few volunteer clients on the side, while you're still employed, in exchange for testimonials and future referrals (assuming it's a good experience).

As a seasoned professional, you may have an advantage that your younger colleagues don't: a network you've spent decades building, including other senior leaders who can hire you.

NOT CUT OUT FOR COACHING? TRY TEACHING

If consulting or coaching doesn't feel like the right fit for you, many executives—seeking an intellectual challenge and looking to give back—explore teaching later in their careers. For nearly a decade, I've taught executive education at business schools around the world, from Duke University's Fuqua School of Business and Columbia University to leading B-schools in Brazil, Russia, Kazakhstan, France, Spain, and more.

Here are three strategies business professionals can follow to position themselves for an adjunct professorship, whether their goal is a part-time side project or a potential career to step into postretirement.

Identify warm leads

As with any job search, you're far more likely to get noticed if someone on the inside can vouch for you. Make a list of connections you know who work, full-time or part-time, at the universities you're interested in approaching (LinkedIn can help). If you can't find any, even tenuous connections can be useful.

Prepare your pitch

Once you've identified who to talk to, you'll need to have a short pitch ready. Don't overwhelm them with information at this point; you'll want to keep this to approximately two paragraphs, so they don't permanently relegate your message to the "I'll read this later" file. The first paragraph should include a short bio that shows why you'd be a good choice to teach for their program. Academic credentials are great, and cite them if you have them, but what matters here is your relevant professional expertise. It's also useful to cite any previous teaching experience you have, whether it's leading internal company workshops or speaking at conferences. The second paragraph should include ideas about what sort of classes or programs you might be able to teach. Take the time to scour their course list, so you have a sense of what they currently offer. You can suggest a mix of preexisting courses you could teach and new ones you could create.

Be ready to produce a CV and syllabus

If you receive a positive response to your inquiry, your contact will ask you to send along two items in advance of meeting. The first item they'll request is a curriculum vitae. CVs are a format popular in academia and are similar to résumés but are much more detailed. Read up on them. The second item your contact will likely request is a syllabus of the course you propose to teach if you're developing it from scratch. You'll need to specify the topics you propose to cover and the order in which you'll teach them, among other things. The *Chronicle of Higher Education* shares a detailed guide on crafting a syllabus.[a]

Teaching college, graduate, or executive education programs can be a rewarding experience, and an opportunity to master new challenges, share your hard-earned knowledge, and gain a valuable new credential.

a. Kevin Gannon, "How to Create a Syllabus," *Chronicle of Higher Education*, https://www.chronicle.com/article/how-to-create-a-syllabus/.

Adapted from "How Executives Can Build a Side Career in Teaching," by Dorie Clark, on hbr.org, December 24, 2018 (product #H04PS0).

As you approach your retirement date, start letting your existing contacts know about your future plans, as they may become your initial clients. Roxann Kriete, the former head of an education nonprofit and the subject of a profile in my book *Reinventing You*, did zero marketing for her new consulting business when she retired, because she'd already received offers for more consulting work than she could handle.

Similarly, DiBernardo began lining up future clients not through any hard-core sales tactics but simply by sharing his plans with longtime colleagues who appreciate his talents. "I've had some relatively senior professionals say that they would hire me in a heartbeat to coach them," he says. "Unbeknownst to me, they say I already have, all these years."

Prepare Your Marketing

Depending on the amount of consulting work you'd like to take on, you may never have to market yourself; your existing network may offer up all the work you'd like. But if you want or need to expand beyond that, make sure you're focused on the right things. Some professionals spend untold hours on surface accoutrements like their business card design or what their slogan should be. (If you can dream up something catchy, great, but no consultant or coach actually *needs* one.)

Recognize the goal of your marketing: establishing a baseline of credibility for when a potential client checks you out. Focus on creating a professional-looking website with testimonials and a social media presence on at least one channel, so that there's a reasonable amount of information about your business online. For instance, you could blog on LinkedIn or another professional site.

Give Yourself a Break

Starting a coaching or consulting business can feel overwhelming, since there's pressure to tackle everything at once. So start slow. Most senior professionals don't want to immediately dive into the hurly-burly of a new career; 52% of respondents to a Merrill Lynch survey reported taking a sabbatical of some length after their official retirement.[4] Even when you're not officially working, you can spend that time preparing in a low-key way, such as building your skills and lining up future clients, as described above.

When you're launching a new consulting venture, it's easy to get distracted by the multiplicity of options— there are plenty of business-building activities you *could* be pursuing. Focus on getting the important things right: Understand what skills you can bring to your clients, leverage your network to find them, and then market just enough to attract the right number of new clients, whether you're looking to build a robust business or simply stay engaged with a few projects on the side.

Consulting and coaching—which are flexible, interesting, and often high prestige—are ideal second careers for retired professionals. Competition is fierce, but by following the steps above, you can lay the groundwork for a fulfilling venture that you can pursue for the rest of your life.

———————

Dorie Clark is a marketing strategist and keynote speaker who teaches at Duke University's Fuqua School of

Business and has been named one of the top 50 business thinkers in the world by Thinkers50. Her latest book is *The Long Game: How to Be a Long-Term Thinker in a Short-Term World* (Harvard Business Review Press, 2021).

NOTES

1. International Coaching Federation, "International Coaching Federation Releases 2020 Global Coaching Study" https://coachingfederation.org/blog/international-coaching-federation-releases-2020-global-coaching-study; Johann Hari, "The Management Consultancy Scam," *The Independent*, August 20, 2010, https://www.independent.co.uk/voices/commentators/johann-hari/johann-hari-the-management-consultancy-scam-2057127.html.

2. Victoria Yore, "Life Coach Certification: Here's How to Find the Best Programs," *HuffPost*, August 10, 2016.

3. Dorie Clark, "Recognized Expert Course," https://learn.dorieclark.com/courses/expert.

4. Merrill Lynch, "Work in Retirement: Myths and Motivations: Career Reinventions and the New Retirement Workscape," 2014, https://agewave.com/wp-content/uploads/2016/07/2014-ML-AW-Work-in-Retirement_Myths-and-Motivations.pdf.

CHAPTER 12

Are You Ready to Serve on a Board?

by Anthony Hesketh, Jo Sellwood-Taylor, and Sharon Mullen

Editor's note: If your calendar and commitments in your working life were too full to carve out some time for board service, retirement can be a great time to put your skills, expertise, and experience to good use for a nonprofit or corporate board.

Corporate boards are under increasing pressure to diversify their ranks—adding more women and minorities, as well as executives with different cultural and functional backgrounds—to better represent the people their

Adapted from content posted on hbr.org, January 31, 2020 (product #H05E3D).

organizations employ and serve. At the same time, the bar for "board readiness" has never been higher: Directors are scrutinized for their ability to understand more complex businesses, demonstrate technical know-how, deliver effective governance, and generate sustainable long-term performance.

What can leaders aspiring to board roles do to prepare and position themselves for success? How does one develop what we call *boardroom capital*?

Unfortunately, the capabilities that power C-suite careers are not the same as those needed to sit around the top table, specifically in a nonexecutive capacity, because you no longer have all the levers of operating power at your fingertips. That is perhaps bad (but not terrible) news for obvious board candidates: They'll simply have to work to develop the right skills. It's unquestionably good news for nonobvious candidates—that is, those who didn't or couldn't ascend to the ranks of top management, which continue to be male- and majority-race-dominated around the world. They will need to work hard too, but they can start on a more level playing field.

As Charlotte Valeur, a Danish-born former investment banker and nonexecutive director at The Bankers Investment Trust PLC and Laing O'Rourke, who has chaired three international companies, as well as the U.K.'s Institute of Directors, told us, "We need to help new participants from underrepresented groups to develop the confidence of working on boards and to come to know that—while boardroom capital does take effort to build—this is not rocket science."

To better understand what makes a director successful, we conducted interviews with more than 50 board members representing some of the world's leading companies. We found that boardroom capital is built on five different types of intelligence: financial, strategic, relational, role, and cultural. The categories might not surprise you, but it is important to understand why all are necessary and to think about how to improve in each area.

Five Types of Intelligence

Financial

Can you talk in numbers, not just in words? Directors cannot fulfill their fiduciary duties without being able to quickly draw an informed opinion on the capital structure of the company, its financial gearing, the sustainability of cash flows, or its risk envelope. These fundamentals have become even more important in the wake of numerous audit-related scandals and increased scrutiny from regulators. But this mandate doesn't require you to have been a CFO or conducted an audit. "It's definitely not a discussion about the technical aspects of accounting," says Crawford Gillies, who serves as senior independent director on the board of Barclays and is chair at other public-sector and private organizations. "For me, the key issue is to be able to interpret an income statement and use that to understand what is going on in the business: what may be going well and not so well." You might want to crack open some old accounting textbooks. But more important is showing that you know enough about the balance sheet to listen attentively to a CFO, ask smart questions, and hold them to account if the financials aren't clear enough.

Strategic

Being fluent in financials is one thing. Can you then translate them into strategy and back again? Ruth Cairnie, former executive vice president of strategy and planning at Royal Dutch Shell and former nonexecutive for Rolls-Royce, who is now chair at Babcock and sits on the board of ABF, outlines the way directors need to think: "Does the strategic thinking pay adequate attention to key trends and external realities? Are we being honest about our competitors' positioning and competitive advantage? Is there a real credible link between the strategy and the projected financials?" Having ensured all the numbers add up, the conversation turns to how the strategic whole might in the future equate to a number *exceeding* the sum of the accounting parts. ESG (environmental, social, governance) issues are now a top priority and an area in which any board aspirant must be knowledgeable. In our research, we identified four different ways that directors have pushed companies to understand, articulate, and measure sustainable value:

- Economies of capital (financial markets)

- Experience (employee and customer value propositions)

- Reciprocity (who you do business with and how)

- Materiality (delivering what you say you are going to deliver)

Boardroom capital requires taking responsibility for looking beyond short-term value realization, to what Joseph Bower and Lynn Paine have described as a company's health, not wealth.[1]

You should also be familiar with new business models and evolving sector-specific strategies (be they services, software, technology or digital, to name a few recent examples) and be comfortable with a faster pace of change than boards have ever faced. Some organizations like the Guardian Media Group in the U.K. boast of being able to tear up and replace their strategic plans every 13 weeks. As Fabiola Arredondo, nonexecutive director at Burberry, Campbell Soup Company, Fair Isaac Corporation (FICO) and FINRA observes, "It used to be that boards would hold a strategic planning session once a year. Now I more typically see boards seamlessly introducing strategic discussions into each board meeting, with a deep dive once or twice a year."

Relational

Stepping up to the board requires you to take a step back. The role is to scrutinize, encourage, and advise, not operate. You need to build successful working relationships with other directors, the company's top executives, and wider stakeholders, each of whom come with their own experience and opinions. In the boardroom, where the pressures are high and the egos large, success turns on the ability to clearly communicate with others and, perhaps more importantly, understand what people are trying to communicate to you.

The ideal, as one of our interviewees described it, is "one big team together, all from different nationalities, different places in the world, different backgrounds, [working as] a unit of people together and enjoying it." But that is not always the reality, Valeur notes, and board relationships require careful management. Being effective involves listening carefully and being able to grasp, process, react positively, and adjust your thinking quickly to the direction of the conversation and to suggestions you may have not previously considered from peers. "The one thing you need to be mindful of coming from a less well-represented group is that you are disrupting the boardroom by simply being who you are," she adds. Her advice is to observe the behavior of more tenured peers while still serving as a diverse voice.

Role

Board members must be clear on their contribution to the conversation. As one experienced boardroom player explained, "We have eight meetings a year. You probably get the opportunity for one, or, if you're really lucky, perhaps two questions per board meeting. That's around 10 questions annually, so you need to make sure you think about what constitutes a material intervention." Ask yourself why you've been picked for the board and on which issues you can add the most value. Mike Clasper of Coats and formerly Which? Limited, notes, however, that the difficult thing about being a non-executive director is not asking a first question probing an underperformance issue or challenging the strategy but knowing when to ask the same question again.

Cultural

Mary Jo Jacobi, former senior U.S. presidential adviser, former senior corporate executive, current board member of The Weir Group and Savannah Resources Plc, and former board member of Mulvaney Capital Management, says that the duty of the board chair and other members is "to create an environment where the executives feel willing to be forthcoming, to admit if something is not going so well, and to seek the board's advice and guidance on how to fix it. It is inappropriate to foster an environment where the execs have to be seen as successful and right and that everything is going great when that is not always the case."

Any director can help their board chair in these efforts. That level of transparency, trust, and rapport flows from careful preparation and orchestration, an ability to quickly evaluate and understand the culture of a group and, if it needs improvement, to develop a plan for finding allies and slowly steering the group toward change. As Ruth Cairnie warns, "I have experienced plenty of organizations where you have very capable people but don't get anything like the best out of them because the dynamics and chemistry are not right."

Building Those Skills

The wisdom of our experienced crowd suggests you do not have to be the finished article before embarking on a boardroom career. But, if becoming a company director is one of your ambitions, you should begin to build board-relevant experience as soon as possible.

Here are a few ways to get started:

- **Financial:** If you haven't already, obtain responsibility for your own P&L; observe carefully how assets, investments, and leveraging combine to drive free cash flows; and listen online to earnings calls.

- **Strategic:** Increase your exposure to your firm's business model and understand how it relates to your strategy and operations and how changes release (and potentially put at risk or destroy) economic value.

- **Relational:** Seek out opportunities to talk with and present to your board and pursue potential decision-making opportunities at the top of internal business units or in external roles. Watch and learn from those you consider expert. Ensure that you enable the success of others on your team and beyond.

- **Role:** Focus on what role you have been chosen to play and where you add the most value. You can practice this in all your meetings and projects. Emulate others who bring that same precision to their work and interactions.

- **Cultural:** Work on your ability to read, get along with, and improve the culture of diverse groups of peers by joining cross-functional, cross-industry, and cross-culture groups.

It also helps to think about what kind of board member you want to be. In our study, we found four common approaches (though the list is not exhaustive, and there remain further variations and combinations including the possibility of board members playing different roles at different times):

- **Police** embrace the increasingly regulatory role board directors are compelled to fulfill; the best ones call executives to account without weighing them down with regulation and red tape.

- **Data junkies** are financially fluent, highly competent, and focused on targets, but should avoid demanding excessive information and acting with too much cold logic in their interactions with peers and executives.

- **Architects** want to lay firm foundations that will outlive the lives of their board tenure; successful ones recognize the delicate balance, structure, and flexibility of short-term returns and longer-term fiduciary and custodial responsibilities.

- **Pilots** see everything from 30,000 feet. They understand and can articulate how value is created, enhanced, protected, and delivered but need vigilance to ensure smooth takeoffs and landings.

Finally, we'd urge you to seek advice from experienced colleagues and contacts, expressing your desire, aspiration, and potential to lead at this level. When sharing your résumé, the content you include should be different from what you have used to date. You should instead signal your potential by outlining your capabilities in each of the five areas of intelligence.

———————

Anthony Hesketh is a senior lecturer at Lancaster University's Management School, U.K. He is the coauthor of *Explaining the Performance of Human Resources Management* and *The Mismanagement of Talent.* **Jo Sellwood-Taylor** and **Sharon Mullen** are the founding directors of Mullwood Partnership, an international search and research business specializing in human resources and nonexecutive board appointments.

NOTE

1. Joseph L. Bower and Lynn S. Paine, "The Error at the Heart of Corporate Leadership," *Harvard Business Review*, May–June 2017, 50–60.

CHAPTER 13

The Leader's Guide to Retirement

by Marc A. Feigen and Ronald A. Williams

"I don't quite know what to do next," said Simon, a media CEO. Simon had been a chief executive for 15 years, and CFO before he was 30. He had turned around private and public companies, quadrupled profits, and quintupled revenue. But, with his company recently sold, Simon was considering retirement. Like many CEOs and leaders, he had no time to plan his retirement—all his focus had been on running the company.

Each year, over 100 CEOs retire from S&P 1000 companies. Even in the most well-oiled succession processes, one piece is almost always missing: preparing the

Adapted from "The CEO's Guide to Retirement," on hbr.org, September 14, 2018 (product #H04JBR).

current CEO for the next phase in their career. "I was so focused on the CEO job, I didn't spend time figuring out what I would do next," says Scott Davis, former CEO of UPS. Bill Weldon, former CEO of Johnson & Johnson, echoes what most CEOs tell us, "I didn't do a lot of thinking about post-employment while I was still the CEO. As a result, I went off the off-ramp at 110 miles an hour and quickly hit zero. Retirement was a black hole."

On average, CEOs step down in their early sixties, relatively young by today's standards. Few have to work for a living. But almost all want to work, and they do. We studied the post-CEO careers of 50 chief executives in the *Fortune* 500 and interviewed 13 of them. Not one retired to the golf course.

While only a few took on another CEO job, almost all of these former CEOs contributed to the U.S. economy and to societal well-being. More than a quarter of them, all past *Fortune* 500 CEOs, became active in private equity. Over half assumed leadership positions at nonprofit organizations, and almost all were philanthropic. Two-thirds served on public boards. Many taught and some wrote books.

After retirement, leaders must grapple with a loss of power, prestige, and immense responsibility. As Ron Sugar, former CEO of Northrop Grumman, told us, "The first few days, it does feel like maybe you've fallen down the elevator shaft."

It can be especially hard on women. As Anne Mulcahy, former CEO of Xerox warns, "There's a special place in hell for retired women CEOs. By the time you are at retirement age, your kids have left the home too. It's double retirement."

Mulcahy further cautions that "the things that work for you as CEO work against you as a retiree, such as being in command and your high energy level." It took her a while to find her footing—she reports "calendar filling." But not for long; as lead director of Johnson & Johnson, chair of Save the Children, and a guest lecturer at Harvard, she found work that gave her purpose and passion. "For me, it wasn't about making money or visibility, but about impact and usefulness."

Any immediate sense of loss is short-lived. Almost every CEO we interviewed reported great satisfaction in their work lives after being CEO. While deeply proud of their accomplishments in the job, they were relieved at breaking free from the corporate calendar.

CEOs and leaders find themselves highly valued after retirement. "It was almost a surprise to me how much you really have to contribute," says Dick Parsons, former chair of Citigroup and former chair and CEO of Time Warner. "But you soon realize: 'I've seen this movie before, I can help here.'"

"It was surprising how quickly opportunity came my way," agrees Doug Hodge, former CEO of PIMCO. "Within weeks of retiring I had opportunities to join a major board, and exciting invitations from venture capitalists to play an active role in fintech companies. I have rebooted myself."

So how do leaders stand up and find fulfillment in their second phase? Most CEOs we spoke to, like Simon, had no time to plan their retirement while running their companies. In our research, we identified some advice to guide retired CEOs and leaders as they plan for Act II.

Plan your off-ramp

Ken Chenault, former CEO of American Express, advises leaders to plan their off-ramp while they are still in the job by "identifying the categories of things that are important to them" but not necessarily the "specific opportunities." Leaders who don't plan risk "falling into the abyss," warns Chenault. "Take the time to plan what is important to you. Don't ignore it. It is very important to be thoughtful." Chenault recommends thinking through one's business, philanthropic, and family priorities. For example, Chenault knew that in his business work, he wanted to focus on digital and technology. "In this way," Chenault says, "when opportunities came my way, I was ready, because I had thought about them." At the beginning of his off-ramp, Chenault did not know exactly what he would do, but he knew what was important to him, which allowed him to move quickly and decisively.

Take your time

The most common error is to rush to fill the void and accept invitations too quickly. As Ron Sugar says, "For the first six months, say no to everything that is offered to you. Usually the first offers you get are not the things you should do." CEOs told us repeatedly that the only thing they got really wrong was to move too fast—which then required unwinding obligations. For example, one CEO accepted a board seat, only to have to wiggle out soon after in favor of a better, larger board opportunity. It would have been wiser to take it slow. Say no often, yes slowly.

Prepare to deal with yourself

Retirement can put even the most self-assured leaders in the unfamiliar position of self-questioning and self-doubt. "It prepares you for dealing with yourself," says one CEO. "You need to know who you are when you're done being CEO," says Mulcahy. She adds: "That means reflecting on aspects of your personality and temperament and sometimes modifying some CEO traits." Parsons told his wife that he could write and teach, and she said, "And what will you do next week?" It took him a while to find his passion. He asked himself what he had wanted to do as a kid. He always wanted to run a jazz club, so he opened one. He also bought a vineyard, reasoning, "In the worst case, I could drink the results!" And he loves it: "There I am in the soil, it's a product, there is dirt under your fingernails, it's tangible." This is deeply personal. "Ask yourself, 'What are the things you will enjoy?'" advises Bill Weldon of Johnson & Johnson.

Partner with your partner

If you have a significant other, it is critical to align expectations—to apply a business term to a family environment. If your spouse has been waiting patiently and now wants to travel, and you want to go back to work, now is the time to develop a shared plan endorsed by your family, or at least understood by them. Every CEO we interviewed planned to spend more time with family and did.

Ken Chenault and his wife scheduled time together for activities important to them.

Assume the role of mentor

There is one feeling of loss that leaders find hard to overcome. It's not the power. It's the people. When asked what he missed from the job, Scott Davis said what many echoed, "The people. I developed a lot of comrades over the years, and you don't see them as much anymore." Leaders who embrace mentorship opportunities find a great way to fill this gap and find fulfillment in passing down their wisdom. As Bill Weldon told us, "We have experienced things other people have not. We can draw on those experiences to help other people." Pat Woertz, former CEO of ADM, sits on the boards of P&G and 3M, is on the Northwestern Hospital board, and advises a startup accelerator in Chicago. She is also mentoring women, "saying yes to more people than I was able to before."

Plan your allocation of time

Write down the hours per day and days per year you want to work. Leave room, as Ron Sugar reminds us, "for surge capacity" as a portfolio of interesting activities can sometimes lead to unpredicted time requirements. Leaving time unscheduled allowed Dick Parsons to assume the role of chair of Citigroup during the financial crisis at the most perilous moment in the bank's history. Later, when the owner of Los Angeles Clippers was censured and removed for racist remarks, Parsons stepped in at the NBA's request to lead the team.

Divide your time between for-profit and not-for-profit. Determine where you want to earn money and where you want to give money. Finally, write down how much time you want to spend with family or personal hobbies. Jeff Kindler, former CEO of Pfizer, notes, "The beauty is you can try things out you haven't been able to before," and he asks, "What are the things in your professional life you never got around to?"

Give back

Very few former CEOs describe their new life as "retirement." Giving back to society is the number one theme we heard. Dick Parsons captured for us the sentiment of many former leaders when he told us, "We owe back to our society. We have to support the platform." Since retiring, Parsons chaired the Rockefeller Foundation and founded two award-winning restaurants to help revitalize the Harlem community in New York City with jazz music and African-inspired cuisine.

Bill Weldon says it best: "The philanthropic side of retirement provides psychic reward and payback far better than any money we receive in our for-profit work." This is the time to build a foundation and begin to distribute your wealth. All of the CEOs we interviewed give back. For example, Ken Chenault chairs the board of the Museum of African American History at the Smithsonian and is a member of the Harvard Corporation. Ron Sugar is trustee of the University of Southern California, director of the Los Angeles Philharmonic Association, member of the UCLA Anderson School of Management's board of visitors, director of the World Affairs Council of Los Angeles, and national trustee of the Boys and Girls Clubs of America. Scott Davis serves as a trustee of the Annie E. Casey Foundation and is a member of The Carter Center Board of Councilors. The 13 former CEOs we interviewed for this article collectively serve on at least 25 philanthropic boards.

With this guidance, leaders can take one of the hardest steps of their career: exiting.

And, as Jeff Kindler told us, "The opportunities are immense. If I had the opportunity to understand what the retirement world would look like before retiring, I would have been able to get my plans together in a matter of months rather than years."

———————

Marc A. Feigen is the CEO and founder of Feigen Advisors, a firm serving CEOs of leading global enterprises. **Ronald A. Williams** is the chair and CEO of RW2 Enterprises and the former chair and CEO of Aetna. He served on the board of directors of American Express and Johnson & Johnson and currently serves on the boards of the Boeing Company and Warby Parker. He is also the chair of Agilon Health and the Conference Board and is an operating adviser to Clayton, Dubilier & Rice.

Make Choices

CHAPTER 14

Deciding on a Drastic Change

by Mark Mortensen

People's motivations for making big career moves—including changing companies, starting new ventures, and leaving the workforce altogether—vary. The pandemic showed some people that remote and flexible work was possible. It prompted others to reevaluate their priorities, particularly around the balance between work and the rest of their lives. And for some, the pandemic came with a large blinking "YOLO" sign that pushed them past fears that kept them from doing what they had always wanted.

Adapted from "A Measured Approach to Making a Drastic Change," on hbr.org, November 3, 2021 (product #H06O9Q).

While far from an exhaustive list, these three examples show how profoundly the pandemic affected how we think about our work. We shouldn't ignore the lessons learned during the pandemic, but we should pressure-test these insights against some of the most obvious biases we struggle with and try to avoid getting trapped on the wrong side of a one-way door.

Why We Should Be Careful

Our decision-making isn't perfect. Nobel laureate Herbert Simon taught us that it's never the fully rational process we'd like to think it is, in part because we're working with incomplete information. Amos Tversky and Daniel Kahneman also pointed out that our own psychology further biases our decisions.[1] Unfortunately, these factors play a large role in people's thinking during times of transition.

I recently spent time with two different managers within the same organization, both of whom were looking to change jobs. Jason wanted to change to a position that allowed for more remote work, citing his increased productivity at home. Helen, in contrast, was feeling disconnected, out of the loop, and isolated as the only member of her team at her location. (All names have been changed.)

In this "grass-is-greener" scenario, both Jason and Helen focused on aspects of their work situations that were particularly vivid and salient for them individually. What both needed was to take some time to think about the whole picture and weigh the pros and cons of each setup. Almost no job-change decision will be unilaterally good or bad—each offers benefits but comes with costs.

As difficult as it is, we need to step outside our immediate contexts to get a more objective view.

Making things even more difficult, the exceptional experiences we've had during the pandemic are affecting our psychology. Data shows a clear link between the pandemic and declines in mental health, which can have a very real impact on decision-making.[2] I spoke to a manager, Chris, who had decided it was time to quit and look for a new job. He told me he felt unmotivated and disengaged in his current role—his work didn't feel meaningful or inspiring and he didn't see a career trajectory that excited him. Further discussion revealed that Chris's concerns were less about his current job but more broadly about his state of mind. He was one of the large percentage of employees experiencing a decline in mental health since the pandemic had begun.[3] In his particular case, discussing with his family helped him realize he was misattributing the cause of his dissatisfaction and that the alternatives he was considering wouldn't meaningfully address what he felt was missing—and in fact, leaving his current organization would take away a support network he had come to rely on.

Before making a big—and potentially irreversible—career decision, take the following steps to make sure you're approaching your decision-making methodically and thinking about how to reduce your personal risk.

Improve Decision Input

First, consider how you can improve the data (and interpretation) going into your decision to yield a more accurate outcome.

Start by quickly refreshing your memory on some of the most common psychological biases to increase your odds of recognizing them when they arise.[4] As someone who has taught about biases for over 20 years, my own decision-making is still affected by biases like:

- **Anchoring:** The tendency for decisions and estimates to be influenced by a starting reference point or "anchor," like the asking price on a car or home.

- **Confirming evidence:** The inclination to favor information that confirms what we already believe, like noticing and believing news stories that align with our views.

- **Availability:** The propensity to over-weight information that's more available in memory because it's more recent, vivid, or emotionally charged. For example, lottery ticket sales tend to increase after a big win is announced.

- **Framing:** The fact that our decisions are profoundly affected by how the decision itself is laid out. For example, we're generally more willing to act to avoid a loss than to achieve a gain.

All of these (and more) are affecting how we approach the critical career decisions we're talking about.

One of my favorite mantras is "outsource what you're bad at"—in this case, that's remaining objective. *Outsource to people* by discussing your decision (and its parameters) with people you know will challenge your assumptions and therefore counter your biases. Devil's advocacy is nothing new and may seem like a given, but particularly in tough situations, we tend to retreat to the safety of discussing our ideas with people we feel confident share our views. Look for someone who has no vested interest in your ultimate decision and remind them that they can only help you by being completely honest.

Outsource to process by putting some structure around how you make your decision. Career decisions are immensely complicated and high stakes—trying to maintain your objectivity while tackling them head-on in their entirety is almost impossible. Instead, take a systematic approach to break them down and outsmart them.[5] For example, before you start to think through it, lay out a road map of how you will evaluate each of the elements in your decision and allocate a time frame for each. This ensures you won't miss—or spend too much or too little time on—any piece of the equation. Importantly, nail down your process *before* starting to think through the decision. That way, you'll avoid inadvertently reworking your process in a way that reaffirms your biases.

Improve Decision Output

Next, consider how you can improve the execution of your decision to reduce the downside risk if your conclusion proves wrong.

Even with the best data and processes, we all still sometimes arrive at what turns out to be a suboptimal conclusion. In light of the Great Resignation, such errors can be particularly costly. Remember, you are your own chief risk officer, so spend some time thinking about how to reduce your exposure if your decision turns out not to be the best one.

One way to do this is to apply a decision-making approach favored by Jeff Bezos and Sir Richard Branson: Divide decisions into one-way versus two-way door decisions.[6] Two-way door decisions are those that are relatively easy to undo. Both Bezos and Branson argue that we shouldn't waste a lot of time deliberating and debating such decisions, but rather try them out and then roll them back if needed. Two-way door decisions are great opportunities for learning. In contrast, one-way door decisions are those that are difficult (if not impossible) to reverse and therefore worth the time and effort to carefully consider and evaluate all options prior to making the decision final.

The first question to ask is whether the career change you're contemplating is a two- or one-way door decision. Maybe you've wanted to start a side business or transition to a new role within your current organization. If you think the change you're considering is relatively easy to abandon or undo, you're in luck—try it out and see what you learn.

However, if that's not the case and you think the costs make the door one-way, ask yourself if there's a way to turn that one-way door decision into a two-way door decision. In one oft-cited example, when Sir Richard Branson was launching Virgin Atlantic, he negotiated a clause in his contract with Boeing that would allow him to return the plane he bought if the airline didn't take off. He ultimately didn't have to exercise that clause, but in negotiating it, he turned the decision from a one-way door into a two-way door.

Is there a way to achieve a similar set of career objectives within the context of your current firm or job? Could you take a sabbatical or transition to part-time to try something out or collect more data? Can you build or strengthen your ties and professional network to increase your options if your intended course of action turns out not to be all that you were hoping?

Recognize that the one-way/two-way door distinction is a decision heuristic—identifying something as one- or two-way is itself a judgment call that depends on your own level of risk tolerance and the costs you're willing to bear. What's too costly to roll back for one person might be within reason for another.

Also keep in mind that you don't need a costless "undo" button to turn a one-way door decision into a two-way door decision. Remember, a one-way door decision is really just one where you think the costs of failure are too large to bear. Reducing your exposure for a decision you can't undo is another way of ultimately making it a two-way decision. So, if you can't walk away from your one-way door decision, see if there are ways to make a bad decision less costly. If you can get the cost low enough that you're willing to incur it if things go wrong and you walk away, you've in effect made it a two-way door decision.

Communicate

Many of these ideas require an open and honest dialogue with your current employer—which may be scary and

153

comes with some risk. Remember, if your current employer truly values you, it's in their best interest to help you resolve your uncertainty and work with you to negotiate a good resolution, as the alternative is a resignation letter that leaves little room for a mutually beneficial solution. One lesson I've learned after watching 20 years of MBAs go through the recruitment process is that we often underestimate our power and ability to outline our own needs, negotiate, and find a workable middle ground. There is no guarantee, but learning how seriously your employer takes your well-being is itself good data to have and very relevant to this whole process.

The pandemic had a profound impact on everyone and sparked some significant realizations and reprioritizations for many. These are important and valid, and should not be discarded. However, we're also all human, operating under the influence of a lot of factors that affect our ability to make decisions. Recognizing and consciously addressing these biases when making critical life decisions are important steps toward making sure we don't find ourselves locked outside on the wrong side of a one-way door.

––––––––––––

Mark Mortensen is an associate professor of organizational behavior at INSEAD. He researches, teaches, and consults on issues of collaboration, organizational design and new ways of working, and leadership.

NOTES

1. Cass R. Sunstein and Richard Thaler, "The Two Friends Who Changed How We Think About How We Think," *New Yorker*, December 7, 2016, https://www.newyorker.com/books/page-turner/the-two-friends-who-changed-how-we-think-about-how-we-think.

2. Macaulay Campbell and Gretchen Gavett, "What Covid-19 Has Done to Our Well-Being, in 12 Charts," hbr.org, February 10, 2021, https://hbr.org/2021/02/what-covid-19-has-done-to-our-well-being-in-12-charts.

3. Alison Abbott, "Covid's Mental-Health Toll: How Scientists Are Tracking a Surge in Depression," *Nature*, February 3, 2021, https://www.nature.com/articles/d41586-021-00175-z.

4. John S. Hammond, Ralph L. Keeney, and Howard Raiffa, "The Hidden Traps in Decision Making," *Harvard Business Review*, September–October 1998, 47–58.

5. Jack B. Soll, Katherine L. Milkman, and John W. Payne, "Outsmart Your Own Biases," *Harvard Business Review*, May 2015, 64–71.

6. Ruth Umoh, "Self-Made Billionaires Richard Branson and Jeff Bezos Reveal How They Make Tough Decisions," CNBC, March 2, 2018, https://www.cnbc.com/2018/03/02/how-richard-branson-and-jeff-bezos-make-tough-decisions.html.

CHAPTER 15

Emotions Aren't the Enemy of Good Decision-Making

by Cheryl Strauss Einhorn

I once gave a keynote address at Cornell University about how to better ensure the success of the decisions we make. I began by polling the audience of about 2,000 people to gauge whether they worry about making mistakes when they face a big decision. A whopping 92% of attendees responded yes.

I then asked the audience to supply one or two words to describe the kind of mistakes that they worry about making. The top responses, captured in a word cloud,

---

Adapted from content posted on hbr.org, September 9, 2022 (product #H0782O).

showed that many of us worry that we rely too much on our gut or our instinct. Specifically, the audience members worried about moving too quickly; being hasty, impetuous, or impulsive; and making emotional decisions.

If so many of us worry that we make mistakes by making decisions too quickly, why do we do it?

When we're faced with difficult and complex decisions, we typically experience difficult and complex emotions. Many of us don't want to sit with these uncomfortable feelings, so we try to get the decision-making over with. But this often leads to poor decisions. We may not truly solve the problem at hand, and we often end up feeling worse. It's an unproductive feedback loop that bookends our decisions with negative feelings.

These emotional bookends, however, can be your secret weapon in making better decisions. The process is as simple as taking the time to identify (1) the emotions you feel as you face your decision, and (2) the emotions you want to feel as you're looking at your decision in the rearview mirror. What do you see? How is your life better for a satisfying decision outcome?

This four-step exercise allows our thinking, or "wizard brain," to check and channel our emotional, or "lizard brain," so that we don't make reactive choices. Here's how it works.

1. Identify the decision you need to make

When we're trying to solve a thorny problem, we often have to sort through a lot of conflicting information—in addition to our feelings. So the first thing to do is to identify what decision you need to make.

Take Charlie, for example. He created a technology to improve hearing while earning his PhD. Now CEO of a neurobiology startup, he's passionate and knowledgeable about everything to do with his invention. But he doesn't have a business background, and he's facing some important business decisions: How does he best use the money he's already raised to move his product to market? How much is it reasonable to spend to develop and test a minimally viable product? How can he raise additional money for his fledgling startup?

Charlie's funders want him to finish his clinical trial and build a product to test in a pilot program. He wants to do right by his investors and meet what he perceives as their very short timeline.

Some of Charlie's advisers and investors have been urging him to find a business-savvy partner. The decision Charlie needs to make is whether he should hire a cofounder with a business background to help him tackle these problems.

2. Identify how you feel about the decision you have to make

Consider your emotions as you contemplate making a big decision. What is the dominant emotion you are feeling? Is it fear? Anxiety? A sense of being overwhelmed or perhaps excitement at the opportunity ahead? Are your feelings based on previous experiences or other sources of information?

Naming our feelings can help create a little space between our emotions and our actions. Gaining that distance allows us to examine the emotion and to acknowledge feeling it, without letting the emotion drive the decision, replacing our conscious thought and agency.

Charlie believes deeply in his product and wants to see this wonderful technology helping people. He feels stuck and unsure how to resolve the decision. He feels anxious and hesitant about his other stakeholders. He is getting conflicting advice from investors and advisers, with some pushing hard to bring on a business-minded partner and others insisting that he can do it himself if he can be more organized with his time.

Creating the distance to identify that he felt stuck was a game changer for Charlie. It helped him realize that, as the CEO, he wasn't stuck at all; instead, he was the sole decision-maker. He also realized that "stuck" wasn't the right word. Instead, he said he felt resistance. When I told him that resistance is not an emotion, but rather a psychological reaction, he was able to analyze further. What he really felt, he said, was discomfort. The clarification was eye-opening. Now he could explore what he felt uneasy about.

3. Visualize your success and how it feels

Imagine that you've made a successful decision. How do you feel now? Do you feel a sense of accomplishment or relief? Do you have a clearer direction for the future? Have you furthered your career, or perhaps strengthened your relationships?

When Charlie imagines hiring a cofounder, he realizes that the feeling of discomfort comes from worries about conflict stemming from having to share decision-making power with someone else. He thought he would feel confidence in the knowledge of the person he hired, but ultimately, he doesn't want to share ownership of the vision that he has dreamed of and sweated over for so many years. Tuning in to his discomfort was a big aha moment, even though it had been there all along.

4. Apply the emotional bookends

Now that you've examined your initial decision and the emotional bookends for it, consider: Have you correctly identified the decision you are making?

Applying the emotional bookending, Charlie realizes that he feels tied in knots because he has conflated several decisions. The decision he needed to make wasn't about hiring a cofounder or not, it was about whether he wants to share ownership of his business. He had assumed that in order to get the business acumen he needed, he would have to bring on a partner, as many of the startups around him seem to have done.

But the exercise of emotional bookending helped him realize that there were other ways to get the business acumen that the company needs. He could hire someone who reports to him or hire a consultant. The business decision is a short-term decision; the partnership is a long-term decision. Not only had he conflated the decisions, but he also hadn't thought through the long-term implications of a partner.

We think we don't have time to invest in the decision-making process—and we definitely don't want to dwell in the emotional discomfort, such as anxiety and frustration, that big decisions bring up. It can feel easier to turn complex decisions over to our emotions—and our lizard brain.

Calling on our wizard brain sounds like magic, but it's not. It requires doing the hard work of slowing down to see the lizard: to name and sit with our emotions. Calling on the wizard brain puts us in partnership with our emotions rather than driven by them.

Emotional bookending helps you name and tolerate your emotions, instead of burying them or running away from them, so that you can better identify—and make— the real decision, the right decision to help you move into your future with clarity and confidence.

———————

Cheryl Strauss Einhorn is the founder and CEO of Decisive, a decision sciences company using her AREA Method decision-making system for individuals, companies, and nonprofits looking to solve complex problems. Decisive offers digital tools and in-person training, workshops, coaching, and consulting. Cheryl is a long-time educator teaching at Columbia Business School and Cornell and has won several journalism awards for her investigative news stories. She's authored two books on complex problem-solving, *Problem Solved* for personal and professional decisions, and *Investing in Financial Research* about business, financial, and investment decisions. Her new book, *Problem Solver*, is about the psychology of personal decision-making and Problem Solver Profiles. For more information, please watch Cheryl's TED talk "When Your Inner Voice Lies to You" and visit areamethod.com.

Retirement Is Hard—Don't Go It Alone

CHAPTER 16

Build Your Retirement Board of Directors

by Priscilla Claman

What does it mean to you to be retired? To work less? Have more control of your time? To finally learn to speak Italian? To cruise the South Pacific in an ocean-going sailboat? Do you scoff, because you can't imagine ever being able to afford retirement or ever *want* to retire? Or are you planning to continue working in some form until you can't anymore?

We know that retirement is no longer the retirement after 40-years-with-the-same-company-and-a-gold-watch situation that it once was. But what is it now? For many of us, it means taking retirement pay or benefits and deciding what to do next. The options are abundant, varied, and possibly overwhelming. It's similar to the open-ended choice you made when you graduated from a university. Who am I? What do I want to do with my life? Where do I want to live? If you were lucky then, you had a group of people who believed in you and your abilities, who mentored you and gave you feedback on your decisions. That's what you need now—an informal board of directors to help you through your retirement decisions.

Why Build a Board to Plan Your Retirement?

You've probably had both formal and informal mentors during your career, especially during the early phase or at critical career transitions—people you talked to before deciding to take on a new job or to get help solving a work problem. As you approach the final seasons of your working life, you may have slowed your networking efforts and think of your retirement as a solo gig. But planning your retirement is better if you don't go it alone. Building a team of folks to tap for support, advice, and insights will help you plan a retirement life that is fulfilling for you.

Creating an informal board of directors for your retirement requires an intentional approach. The members don't have to meet but only agree to help you as you think about your retirement, test ideas, make choices, and transition into your new reality.

Inviting people to help you should be low key and direct, like, "I'm looking into retirement options. I really respect your opinion. Can I run some ideas by you from time to time?"

With your goal in mind and your ask prepared, here's who to add to your retirement-planning board.

The officers

There are four kinds of people who should be on your board of directors no matter what you are interested in exploring as you contemplate slowing down or stopping work completely.

Close friends and family

The first people you should add to your retirement-planning board are those who will be most impacted by your retirement decisions, usually friends and family. You probably have already started to talk about retirement with your close friends and family members. If you have one, your partner is an easy choice for your board, but there may be others close to you to consider such as your parents and your adult children.

Financial adviser(s)

Stepping away from a regular source of income requires financial advice from someone reliable. If you work for a large organization, make an appointment with your company's benefits professional. If you have a financial adviser, make an appointment with her, too. If you don't have one, seek out an independent financial planner to develop a retirement plan. These experts will help you decide how much money you will have in retirement and may help you decide when to retire as well.

Health adviser(s)

This stage of life is not without its health challenges, so you need to add folks to your retirement-planning board who can help you understand your health insurance options. Any financial adviser can help you decide what kind of health insurance you need, when to join Medicare if that is an option where you will live, or what sort of private supplements you may need to add to your country's universal health insurance. But you'll probably want to check in with your primary care doctor to get a wellness checkup and input on how your diet or exercise needs might change after retirement.

Legal adviser

Finally, you should consider adding an attorney for a will, a health-care proxy, or any other legal advice, especially if you are stepping away from a family business or partnership.

As you refine your retirement choices, these four basic members of your board of directors—people close to you, your financial adviser(s), your health adviser(s), and an attorney—are people you will want to continue to check in with.

The specialists

How you choose to build out your retirement board of directors beyond the officers depends in part on what direction you choose. Basically, you'll want to add people who know you and can support you during your search, like current mentors or work colleagues, and add people from the new fields you're considering to understand what that option is like. This is true whether retiring for you means working fewer hours and assuming a reduced role at a new job or whether it means volunteering or spending more time with a favorite hobby. Test your ideas by talking to people in the field you're considering. On your board, you will always need some "from" people and some "to" people, even if the "from" people are venture capitalists and the "to" people are potters. Here's some ideas for building out your board and tapping it for input, based on how you choose to retire.

Quitting work cold turkey? Include former colleagues

Some people decide to retire abruptly and play golf. The temptation then is to add a golf pro to your board of directors and forget your work network. But you should hedge your bets for a year or two. Some people get bored without something more structured to do after about a year. So, for a few years, keep on your board of directors two or three people from your working life who know you and what you are good at, so you don't start from zero if you have retirement remorse and want to search for something else.

Transitioning to a new career or new location? Include new mentors

Other people turn the page by retiring from their old career and making the transition to a new one instead of fully stopping work. A successful sales and marketing executive loved her vacation house and its community and thought that being a real estate agent in the community would be a great option to supplement her retirement income. She talked to real estate agencies there and sold herself to one whose CEO mentored her through the licensing process and got her off to a good start. Along with the CEO, she put two local friends on her board of directors who helped her connect more deeply with the year-round community.

To translate this realtor's approach to your context, figure out if you need to supplement your retirement pay, find an activity you love that you can use to earn that income, and invite to your board people from your previous work life who can vouch for your skills, as well as people from your new activity to help you make the transition.

Easing into retirement? Bring your manager along

Easing into retirement is what the head of graphics and communications at a media-related nonprofit chose. When he retired, he persuaded management to give him a three-month contract to complete a major project. That was the start of his small consulting practice. He put his manager on his informal board of directors for a reference and added two colleagues from other media organizations and a person from a relevant professional association. With a strong board of directors and in control of his time, he could expand or reduce his consulting hours by taking on fewer projects. Initially, he cleared the month of July each year for a family vacation. Ultimately, he chose to retire completely eight years later.

To understand how easing into retirement could work for you, think about your professional skills. Are there skills you particularly enjoy using? Are they something you could sell or volunteer to another employer? Are you a corporate recruiter? You could be a headhunter. Are you a retiring CFO? How about marketing your skills and experience to other firms in your industry? Add people from professional services firms to your board of directors to see if this direction is feasible for you.

How to Build a Board If You Don't Know What You Want to Do Next

If you're like many people who put off thinking about retirement because they don't know what they want to do, or when the right time to retire is, or even if they can afford to retire, it's time to revisit your officers. They can give you the foundational information you need to help you answer your questions. If you are happy with your work, you certainly don't need to decide now, but if you are feeling trapped in your job or organization and are getting more and more cynical, you should consider retirement as a transition away from what's making you unhappy.

And, yes, at the beginning, choosing a retirement approach will feel a little like the "now what?" you probably felt when you graduated from university. But you are not the same as you were then. You have a reputation, skills, connections, and experience you didn't have then. Use your connections and colleagues to find the right people for your board of directors, to help you explore some choices, and when you have some options, to help you choose between them.

For example, a prominent marketing executive didn't think about retirement while he was working, so he gave himself a year to figure out what he wanted to do after he retired. His informal board of directors recommended he decompress with a vacation. His trip to the Great Barrier Reef in Australia got him interested in climate change. Back home, he helped his daughter's climate-change nonprofit refine its message. He used his board of directors to network with state legislators and put one of them on his board. Within a year, he had found his new direction as a climate-change lobbyist.

Focus on Your Future

Remember when you went to college as a first-year student and found yourself no longer the high and mighty high school senior? Retirement can feel like that—a sudden demotion. Some people continue to look backward in retirement, refusing to let go of their preretirement status.

To retire well, you have to look forward. If you go around saying, "I *was* a human resources executive," or "I *was* the COO of a tech company," your focus is on the past. You will have a hard time recruiting people to your board of directors, identifying opportunities, and meeting people who can help you craft your future.

To look forward, craft an "I *am* . . . " statement, even if you haven't decided yet what you want to do. An "I am" statement will make it far easier to introduce yourself to new people, expand your board of directors—and your way of thinking about yourself.

Here are several examples of future-focused "I am" statements:

- "I am a retired logistics manager looking for an opportunity to make a contribution to an organization like yours."

- "I am a retired CEO looking to become a director of a nonprofit in the education sector."

- "I am retired and working to improve my golf game."

Try on your "I am . . . " statement until it is comfortable. Change it when it isn't comfortable. Write out possibilities. Practice with friends and your board of directors. Or create a couple of "I am . . . " statements for different occasions. Then, when you have made the transition to whatever your retirement looks like for you, you can say with pride, "I am a real estate salesperson in one of the most beautiful towns in America." Or, "I am a consultant to media firms in design and communications." Or, "I am enjoying living in a seaside community, where all my friends and family come visit me."

However you define your retirement, creating your own board of directors will help you through the process. Then, when you have made it through your transition to retirement, pay it forward by serving on someone else's board of directors.

———————

Priscilla Claman eased into retirement from her Boston-area firm that offered career coaching and career management services, only to be brought back into the fray by her HBR editor and the cool opportunity to write about using a board of directors to craft the right retirement. She is also a contributor to the *HBR Guide to Getting the Mentoring You Need* (Harvard Business Review Press, 2013) and the *HBR Guide to Managing Up and Across* (Harvard Business Review Press, 2014).

CHAPTER 17

Relationships and Your Retirement

by Teresa M. Amabile

Although your retirement is, most definitely, *yours*, it isn't yours alone. In sometimes profound ways, it is your partner's, your family's, and your friends', as well. The people you're closest to can't help but be affected by the dramatic life change *you* experience when you leave your working days behind, and you cannot help but be affected by them either. Many aspects of your life will change with retirement, including the structure of your days, the ways you use your time, the groups you belong to, and your relationships. Of all these, relationships may be the most important; according to past research, relationships are a key contributor to people's well-being in retirement, influencing emotional health, cognitive functioning, and even physical health.[1] And, according to new research that my team and I have been doing, maintaining certain existing relationships and developing new ones can help ease your transition to retirement, bringing joy and support to the later years of your life.

This chapter offers coping strategies and questions to consider based on real stories from the research that my team has been conducting over the past eight years. Among other data collections, we've followed 14 people with multiple interviews across their retirement transitions, to learn about their psychological and social experiences in as much depth as possible.[2] By following people across time, and supplementing our findings with onetime interviews of another 69 older adults (some still working and some recently retired), we were able to look deeply into the dynamics of relationships, how they can change—both for better and for worse—when people retire, and what retirees can do to improve their relationships.[3]

Consider Jay and his wife, Debra, who had quite different views of what they wanted in retirement. I interviewed Jay, a management consultant, 10 times across more than six years—as he approached retirement, retired, and experienced the early years of his retirement. Debra wanted to have more one-on-one time with Jay and also continue the many social and volunteer activities she'd been doing in the years since they became empty nesters. He, by contrast, longed to plunge back into a youthful passion he'd had for hot rods, spending hours alone in his workshop tinkering with the car he'd just bought, and exploring the local hot rod club. These differences caused a number of misunderstandings, hurt feelings, and arguments in the first postretirement year—for example, when Debra wanted Jay to head out for a romantic picnic and he was deeply into some intricate metalworking, or when he was settling in to watch a favorite TV show just as she was about to set up lunch in the den for her book group. Realizing that they needed help steering their relationship through this fraught time, they entered into couples counseling. With patience, hard work, and perseverance, they found compromises that led, eventually, to some of the happiest times of their marriage—giving each other time and space each week, but also rediscovering each other as they explored the country together on road trips. Even so, divergent expectations about what retirement life should be, and their resultant disappointments with each other, never fully disappeared.

Simon had a very different spousal experience. His second wife, Helen, recently retired from her career as a nutritionist, had been urging him to retire, and he couldn't have been more eager to join her—yet his alimony payments necessitated that he keep working for two more years. From the day he finally retired, they embraced retirement life with gusto, growing closer through leisurely breakfast conversations, planting and harvesting a garden together, and volunteering for political causes about which they were passionate. Simon and his wife experienced a smooth and easy transition of their spousal relationship.

Margaret, the most introverted of the people we've been following, had been widowed several years earlier, but hoped to enjoy this phase of life with Trudy, her closest friend for decades, and, if possible, make some new friends. Although she approached people tentatively, worried about each interaction, she eventually found that retirement gave her the time and the emotional bandwidth to develop some friendships that became mutually supportive and brought new enjoyment to her life, even as she deepened her relationship with Trudy.

Relationship Dynamics in Retirement

The story of your own relationships with your partner or family members or friends, as you transition into retirement, may not be as difficult as Jay's, but it's unlikely to be as smooth as Simon's either; most likely, it will be somewhere in between, a mix of struggles and satisfactions, like Margaret's. To a considerable extent, what you do before, during, and after retiring will make a difference. You certainly can't design everything about the number and quality of your relationships in retirement, but there is much that you can do to shape them to a comfortable fit. Of course, what makes for a comfortable fit will depend on who you are and what you want from retirement life—whether that's a sense of meaning and purpose in how you spend your time; a stream of enjoyable days, weeks, months, and years (with "enjoyable" defined by you); relaxation and refreshment; self-discovery; deep connection with other people; learning and growing; or something else. Figuring that out will serve as a great starting point for thinking productively about how your relationships might facilitate or undermine your fulfillment of those dreams.

Your partner

If there is one person with whom you most closely share your life, make them part of your retirement story from the very beginning. The vast majority of the people we interviewed discussed the financial aspects of retirement with their partners before deciding on a retirement date. But, to our surprise, many didn't go beyond that to discuss what their lives would actually be like, day to day, month to month, after retirement. We suspect that if Jay had been honest with himself and Debra about his desire to spend much of his time engaged in hot rod activities, their postretirement relationship would have gotten off to a much better start, much sooner. Simon and Helen did have those discussions, together developing a few specific ideas about how to spend time in that first postretirement year; when the day finally came, their jointly developed plan for daily life together was ready to go, with enough flexibility to allow for unexpected challenges and opportunities.

It's difficult to overstate the importance of discussing with your partner, in advance and at some level of detail, what retirement life will be like day to day—with at least a few different options that appeal to both of you—so you can pivot in the face of events over which you have no control. The case of Lawrence and Cynthia serves as a cautionary tale on this score. They did plan retirement life together, in a very general way, jointly developing their retirement dream of moving to a distant state where their son and his wife lived, to help care for their beloved toddler grandson a few days a week. Unfortunately, they hadn't considered what to do when they weren't with that grandson and his parents, what other relationships they might need in their lives besides that little family. After moving, they joined no groups or activities in their new community, developed no friendships, and didn't even get to know their neighbors. When their son's marriage fell apart in the year after they moved, severely limiting their time with the grandson, their problem drinking spiraled into serious alcoholism. Only by entering a long-term residential rehab program, at the end of their third postretirement year, and staying involved in a 12-step program, were Cynthia and Lawrence able to regain their health, save their marriage, and eventually create a happy retirement full of healthy relationships. In retrospect, Lawrence said that, had they established the practice of talking through the details of their daily lives early on and developed plans for building community, they could have better weathered the storm that life threw their way.

If one of you will be retiring before the other, consider how your lives will work, at a fairly granular level, during that interim time.[4] Who will do the cooking, housework, and household errands? Simon and Helen had agreed that she would do the lion's share of that work until he retired, at which point they would divide up the chores. Irene, who retired in her mid-60s, before her husband was ready to retire, understood—and embraced—the responsibility she would have for overseeing the renovation of their summer cottage into their full-time retirement home. Indeed, she relished the opportunity to make that space her own and find her own place in their new community while her husband was still busy with his job. If the two of them had not come to this mutual understanding beforehand, however, either or both of them might have ended up feeling resentful.

Your family

Your retirement will impact your adult children and members of your extended family, and vice versa. You can shape that impact by proactively thinking about what you'd like those relationships to become. Simon's daughter, who lived in another state and had two young children, had never really accepted Helen. Before retirement, out of deference to his daughter's feelings, he would always travel alone to visit her. However, realizing that he wanted his marriage to take center stage in his life after retirement, he gently but firmly told his daughter that, from now on, he would visit with Helen or not at all. His daughter relented, and Helen soon developed a strong, loving relationship with her stepdaughter's entire family.

Before his retirement, Jay didn't have much to say about his adult son, describing their relationship as fine but distant because his son's life was so busy. But, to Jay's delight, his rekindled passion for hot rods led his son to develop the same interest. They took road trips together, forging a new, closer bond. That bond held both of them steady when Debra died unexpectedly during a routine surgery; father and son found comfort in each other as they mourned.

More-distant relatives can also be important in retirement, so consider which of those relationships you might want to nurture. Douglas, who had grown up in a different country, longed to connect more regularly with members of his far-flung extended family after retiring. He and his wife planned a series of trips in their first postretirement year, with rest stops at home in between. As a result, he not only deepened some cherished relationships that had been conducted electronically, but even reconnected some of those relatives with each other.

Your friends

Retirement brings opportunities to discover novel joys and sources of support in friends old and new. Having read that relationships are important to healthy aging, and aware that she would have to fight her natural tendency to curl up on the sofa at home with her pets and her books, Margaret sought out friendships through new activities. By taking classes at her local gym and joining a weekly spirituality group, she soon developed a small but vibrant set of friends in whom she found great enjoyment—and, later, when her health began to fail, great support.

Irene had had a number of good friendships with work colleagues and neighbors, and she expected that those friendships would continue after she moved to the summer cottage. To her surprise, however, those relationships began to fall away in the first months after she retired, and she felt all right letting those friends go, now that she had less in common with them. Simultaneously, to her delight, daily walks in her new neighborhood, along with art classes she had joined to pursue a hobby that had long attracted her, led naturally to new acquaintances—some of which eventually developed into close friendships.

How to Think and Talk About Your Retirement

What does all of this mean for you and your own retirement? It means that you must think carefully about your key relationships as you move toward and live within your retirement years.

The following questions will get you started in considering how you might want to shape your relationships. Reflect on them yourself and then, as appropriate, discuss them with the most important people in your life:

- Who are you at this time in your life, in terms of your strongest identities, traits, preferences, and motivations? Who do you wish to become in retirement?

- What are your hopes, goals, expectations, and fears about retirement life?

- Given who you are, who you wish to become, and what you want in retirement life, are there certain relationships that you want to maintain or deepen, to help you get there? How might you accomplish this, through real time spent together, distance communication, or both? Are there relationships you want to let go? Others you want to move in a new direction? Consider your current and possible future needs for both friendly, casual connections and deep, intimate relationships, as well as your needs to both give and receive tangible help and support.

- Do you need to refresh your life through new relationships—or new activities that might lead to new relationships? If so, how? Consider neighbors and fellow group members (such as church congregants), especially those who are also retired. What activities might you start or resume to meet people who might become new friends? Start with chats after church or the club meeting and, if you hit it off, plan to meet for a meal or walk together. Even (perhaps especially) if you're an introvert, develop what one retired person calls a "Yes day" mentality. If someone you like invites you to do something that doesn't require a big commitment (like checking out a bocce group or a book reading), just say yes. It could lead to a new friendship.

- Do you have some reasonably clear ideas about how you'll spend your days in the first months and years postretirement, and how congruent are those plans with those of your partner and the other important people who are implicated in them?

- What expectations do the key people in your life have about your retirement, and what expectations do you have of them? Will your still-working partner expect you to handle all household matters after you retire? If you're retiring simultaneously, have you discussed your needs and preferences for daily schedules, time together versus apart, division of labor, and using the spaces in your home when you're both there? Do you have dreams for how to spend your time in retirement that might not mesh with, say, your daughter's hopes that you'll provide childcare for the grandchildren, or your partner's desire for world travel?

- If you're planning a major postretirement change, such as moving to a new community, what are the implications for the important people in your life, and what might you (and they) do if the change doesn't work out as you'd hoped? Can you (and they) envision attractive options together?

Reflect on and discuss questions like these, with kindness toward yourself and the other people in your life, ever mindful that both you and they will be exerting mutual influence on your relationships. Consider how you will react to expected and unexpected turns in those relationships, in a way that stays true to yourself and your needs in retirement. As our research shows, approaching your relationships with both attention and intention can help you avoid some painful pitfalls of retirement and allow you to enjoy some of its sweetest fruits.

——————

Teresa M. Amabile is a Baker Foundation Professor at Harvard Business School and the coauthor of *The*

Progress Principle (Harvard Business Review Press, 2011). Her current research, about which she and her co-researchers are writing a book, investigates how people approach and experience the transition to retirement.

NOTES

1. One recent study found that cultivating friendships in retirement can lead to lower levels of depression: B. L. Kail and D. C. Carr, "Structural Social Support and Changes in Depression During the Retirement Transition: 'I Get By with a Little Help from My Friends,'" *Journals of Gerontology: Series B* 75, no. 9 (2020): 2040–2049. Another found that supportive relationships can lead to a greater sense of purpose in older adults: S. J. Weston, N. A. Lewis, and P. L. Hill, "Building Sense of Purpose in Older Adulthood: Examining the Role of Supportive Relationships," *Journal of Positive Psychology* 16, no. 3 (2021): 398–406. Particularly intriguing results emerged from a study of the effects of positive partner relationships on personality change in older adults. This study found that as positive support from the relationship partner increased, there were increases in adaptive personality orientations, including higher levels of conscientiousness, extraversion, agreeableness, and openness to experience, and lower levels of neuroticism: P. L. Hill, S. J. Weston, and J. J. Jackson, "The Co-Development of Perceived Support and the Big Five in Middle and Older Adulthood," *International Journal of Behavioral Development* 42, no. 1 (2018): 26–33. In a study of more than 2,500 American adults over age 65, more frequent contact with friends at one point in time was associated with better memory, executive function, and language two to four years later: L. M. Meister and L. B. Zahodne, "Associations Between Social Network Components and Cognitive Domains in Older Adults," *Psychology and Aging* 37, no. 5 (2022): 591–603. A different study found similar effects of frequency of interaction with friends: N. Sharifian et al., "The Longitudinal Association Between Social Network Composition and Episodic Memory in Older Adulthood: The Importance of Contact Frequency with Friends," *Aging & Mental Health* 24, no. 11 (2020): 1789–1795. A recent study using data on a large sample of older adults over a 10-year period found that those with better social relationships at the beginning of the study period had better cardiometabolic health 10 years later: K. Shartle et al., "Social Relationships, Wealth, and Cardiometabolic Risk: Evidence from a National Longitudinal Study of US Older Adults," *Journal of Aging and Health* 34 (2022): 1048–1061.

2. The research team I lead includes Lotte Bailyn, professor emerita at MIT Sloan School of Management; Marcy Crary, professor emerita at Bentley University; Douglas T. Hall, professor emeritus at

BU Questrom School of Business; and Kathy Kram, professor emerita at BU Questrom School of Business.

3. Of the 47 retired people we interviewed (including those we interviewed repeatedly), the average age of retirement was 63, with a very wide range from 52 to 70 years old. At the time we interviewed them (which varied from days after they retired to seven years after they retired), 62% were married, 26% were single, 6% were not married but in a committed relationship, 4% were widowed, and 2% were separated. We did not ask about sexual orientation.

4. Of the 32 retired people we interviewed who were married or in a committed relationship, 50% had partners who were still working at the time they retired.

CHAPTER 18

Retirement Is Stressful

by Ruth C. White

For many of us, retirement is a dream. At the start of our careers, we don't often give it more thought than enrolling in a savings plan or filling out tax forms. When retirement age grows closer to becoming a reality, we joke about it, daydream about it, and perhaps worry about it. Will we be lucky enough to have the money, good health, and companionship of family and friends to enjoy our golden years? For those of us who have built our lives around work, the transition to not working can be stressful. In your working life, you move projects forward, crossing off items from an endless to-do list. You feel accomplished, receive praise and recognition, and earn economic rewards. In your retired life, you may be surprised to endure a big and stressful adjustment, as you transition to personal projects and a to-do list of activities that no one but you will know about. You may feel less useful and important when you are no longer speaking to audiences about your work, making that big sale, or getting that promotion you worked so hard for. You may feel gratified to finally make progress on those household, family, and personal tasks that you didn't have time for when you were working. When it comes to retirement, you likely won't know how it will feel until you actually get there.

What we do know is that more people are facing retirement than ever before. According to the World Health Organization (WHO), every country in the world is experiencing an increase in the size and proportion of the elderly in their population.[1] WHO predicts that by 2030, one in six people globally will be over the age of 60, and this population is expected to double by 2050.

This demographic shift, known as "population aging," means an increase in the number of retirees and a corresponding increase in the length of time that people will be retired. Retirement is more than the absence of work; it can also deeply impact your identity, relationships, and status, which can be stressful. So there are more of us growing older and living longer than ever. But it's not all golden. There is conflicting data about the impact of stress on the mental health of retirees. One meta-analysis of 11 studies found the prevalence of depression among a total of 6,111 retirees to be 28%.[2] One study found a 6% to 9% decline in mental health over an average postretirement period of six years, and it also found evidence that this impact may be stronger for people who retire involuntarily (understandably so, since being in control of the conditions under which you retire will be much less stressful than feeling "forced out").[3] Another meta-analysis of 60 data sets, totaling 557,111 subjects, found that retirement *reduced the risk of depression* by almost 20%.[4] Finally, an article from Harvard Medical School reported that doing too little *or* too much in retirement can have the same symptoms: depression, anxiety, memory impairment, loss of appetite, and insomnia.[5] Although depression and anxiety are not necessarily always an outcome of stress, high levels of consistent stress are a risk factor and trigger for mental health conditions like anxiety and depression.[6] While the research is conflicting and confusing, and everyone has their own context, identifying your sources of stress can help you take proactive steps to prepare for this significant life transition from an emotional and psychological standpoint, helping you reduce and manage your stress and enjoy a more positive retirement.

Sources of Stress

Of course, the circumstances of your retirement will impact the way you experience the stress of this major life event. Your retirement-related stress may be tied to the way in which you retire, the change to your daily structure, the impact on your relationships, feelings of isolation, and financial concerns.

How you retire

In an ideal world, we get to pick the circumstances and time we retire. If you have planned for your retirement and things are going accordingly, you may have more excitement than fear or anxiety. But that ideal is not available to all of us. If you have to retire before you wanted to because of an illness, have to take care of family members, or because of a layoff, you may experience a lot of stress because you were not expecting it.

Structure of your days

Even if everything is exactly as you planned or dreamed, the shift from a 40- to 60-hour workweek to 40 to 60 hours of free time can be a challenging adjustment, especially in the first few weeks or months of retirement. The change of pace takes getting used to, even if you have set plans for classes you'll take, trips you have booked, and activities you'll join.

Changes to relationships

Although the pandemic made working from home a norm for so many, you may feel isolated and disconnected when there is no team to check in with and share happy hours, watercooler conversations about sports and headlines, and corporate events with free bev and bites.

Feeling of isolation

Retirement can definitely engender feelings of FOMO—fear of missing out. You may see your still-working colleagues going on business trips together and getting big promotions and wonder if you made the right decision to retire when you did. Also, if you live alone as many seniors do, you may have feelings of loneliness now that you're not regularly connecting with others for work. According to a study from the Pew Research Center, more U.S. seniors live alone than anywhere else in the world; 27% of U.S. adults over 60 live alone, compared to 16% in the rest of the 130 countries studied.[7] Older women are almost twice as likely as their male counterparts to live alone, partly due to women living longer and marrying men who are older than them. And lots of research shows that social isolation negatively impacts the mental *and* physical health of seniors.[8]

Financial concerns

Money is a common source of stress for many people at different stages of life. Financial stress can increase in retirement, when people stop working and therefore relinquish their ability to grow their savings. According to a CNBC feature on retirement, 37% of Americans feel unprepared or unsure if they are on track for retirement.[9] One big concern, especially for Americans, is having enough money to cover health-care costs, as our health naturally declines with age. One survey found that more than a third of Americans are concerned that they won't be able to cover health-care costs in the next year.[10] If you still have debt such as a mortgage or student loans (for yourself or your children), you may also have some anxiety about carrying these debts into retirement. Last, as life expectancy increases, many people wonder if their savings will last for the remainder of their lives. And current economic downturns only exacerbate those fears. If you traveled or entertained as part of your job, it may also be stressful to realize that from now on your travel and fancy meal expenses are coming out of your own fixed-income pockets. So financial preparation for retirement is integral to your emotional and psychological health.

Coping with Stress During the Phases of Retirement

According to Robert Atchley's classic book, *The Sociology of Retirement*, there are seven stages of retirement, and depending on where you are in the "retirement life cycle," the sources of stress may differ.[11] We'll discuss the first six phases to help you plan your retirement. Knowing that the phases exist will help you identify them and manage your response during them. (We won't address here the last stage—termination—when people are close to the end of life.) People generally go through these phases of retirement in the order in which they are listed, but each person goes through them at their own pace, and some may skip certain stages, such as the disenchantment and reorientation phases, depending on their orientation toward life. Sometimes a change in circumstances can cause a jump backward or forward. For example, inheriting money in later stages may bring people back to the honeymoon stage or forward to the stability stage. Or a more negative experience such as the diagnosis of a chronic illness may cause a shift to the disenchantment or reorientation phases.

The first stage is **preretirement**. This usually takes place in the five to 10 years before you plan to retire, when most people start to focus on financial planning. This may mean downsizing to a smaller home after your children have left. For others, it may mean planning for a change in where they live geographically. For example, if you live where winters are long and cold, you may decide to move permanently or temporarily (aka snowbirds) to where the climate is more favorable. The stress associated with this time of your work life may be rooted in a generalized anxiety about getting or feeling older, wondering if you have enough money saved, and not having a concrete plan for retirement.

Cope: To address this source of stress, focus on making a clear and concrete plan for your future. Write down your dreams for retirement, meet with a financial planner to see how realistic your goals are, and take steps to make those dreams come true. It may also help to focus on healthier eating and living so that you plan for a healthy and long life in retirement. Consuela Chapman, a licensed therapist and health coach in North Carolina, advises that you take advantage of any counseling offered through your organization's employee assistance programs to help you prepare for your new normal of retirement.

The second—and shortest stage—is **retirement day**. This is the actual day of your retirement, which your organization and colleagues may celebrate. It may mean a gift of some kind and maybe a party at the office or a fancy restaurant. Many people look forward to this day as it marks the before and after of their work lives. And though the actual day may be celebratory, there may be stress related to setting the date and telling your boss and family. And if you feel like you're being pushed out, this day may not be so celebratory.

Cope: The best way to deal with this day is to reflect on your career achievements, which may be the focus of your retirement speech or the goodbye email you send to colleagues. You can even do this just for yourself to feel a sense of accomplishment. Another way to make this day as positive as possible is to list at least three things for which you are grateful as you say goodbye to work and start a new stage of life.

The third stage is the **honeymoon phase**, when you do a lot of the things you always wanted to but did not have the time or freedom: impulse trips to see family or to explore new places, fully indulging your hobbies—whether gardening, painting, or knitting; learning a new language just because; or volunteering for your favorite cause. The honeymoon phase is also when you may relish loss—the loss of waking to an alarm clock, a painful commute, a calendar so packed with meetings that you didn't have time to eat or grab a coffee. There is no determined length of time for this phase, as it really depends on your emotional and psychological reaction to retirement and all the activities you planned to do.

Cope: As this stage is labeled the honeymoon phase, it is the least stressful period of retirement, so soak it up. You love retirement and the new life you have worked so hard for and may have feelings of joy, satisfaction, excitement, and achievement. To extend this period, it may help to journal your positive feelings so that you can refer to them when you need an emotional boost as you move through less positive phases. While things are good, you may want to prepare for the future by creating an advance directive. Vanessa Souza, a social worker with more than 15 years of experience working with the elderly in the San Francisco Bay Area, says, "My number one piece of advice for retirees is to immediately identify who will be both your financial and your medical power of attorney, should you need someone to make decisions on your behalf, and who is going to help you get what you need if you are physically or cognitively unable to do it yourself." She finds that most people don't want to think about this when things are going well, but an advance directive is just one more way to have peace of mind going forward.

Next is the **disenchantment phase**, when you start wondering if "this is it" for the rest of your life. The emotional high of the freedom to do as you please starts to wane and the downside of too much freedom and too little structure starts to kick in. You may start feeling anxiety about only spending money while not earning money. You may face yet another unplanned day with dread instead of adventure. You may ache for a goal or a sense of accomplishment. And as Chapman says, "Individuals who have recently retired and are not adjusting as well to the change may begin to feel anxious and or depressed. It's not uncommon for retirees to go through the grief cycle as well. Leaving a career and the relationships established is a loss."

Cope: One way to deal with the stress of this phase is to focus on the things you enjoy about retirement and try to solve the parts that you don't. Go back to that list of career achievements, your gratitude list, and read journal entries from the honeymoon phase to help shift to a more positive mindset. Be proactive in connecting with friends and family to do things you enjoy together. And if you really miss working with a great group of people on a shared goal, sign up for a volunteer opportunity where you collaborate on making a difference in someone's life; that may mean joining a nonprofit board, delivering Meals on Wheels, or volunteering in a K–12 classroom. Hobbies and volunteering have been found to improve both mental and physical health of retirees.[12] If you're seeking to get out of your retirement rut, consider joining the Peace Corps or taking a volunteer trip abroad. And if you find that feelings of grief and loss are persistent, find a mental health professional to help you through that process.

The fifth stage is **reorientation**. For some people, this can be the most challenging stage, as you figure out your new identity and start to acclimatize to a new way of life. You want to be able to answer the perennial question about what you do without any anxiety and feel a sense of purpose in this new life you have created for yourself.

Cope: To maneuver through this period, create a routine that works for you. Go to bed and wake at the same time every day to regulate your circadian rhythms, and exercise to keep your bones and muscles strong, maintain a healthy weight, and reduce the risk of chronic illnesses. You should also include regular meetups with friends and family to be socially connected and to boost your emotional resilience. To provide a sense of purpose, look for an opportunity to engage in your community in a way that feels meaningful.

The last and final stage we'll address here is the **stability stage**, also known as the **reconciliation stage**. At this point, you have settled into a life that gives you feelings of purpose and fulfillment. Like everyone else you will have ups and downs emotionally and psychologically, but you have ways of dealing with these changes without much trouble. Like any other period of life, this stage of retirement won't always be smooth sailing and you will have psychological and emotional ups and downs. You may have to deal with the death of friends and family, illness of children or partner, or downturns in your economic fortune.

Cope: Lean into the coping strategies that work for you that you developed in the earlier stages. Keep these strategies in rotation as needed. At this stage you may want to consider recording the story of your life as a legacy for your children or grandchildren or as a historical record. Writing or recording the story of your life will give you a sense of legacy. And regularly sharing these stories with family and community can keep you connected in very powerful ways. You may even explore the idea of writing and publishing a memoir.

No matter what stage of retirement you are in, if you are feeling overwhelmed, or find that you are experiencing extended periods of anxiety or depression or other mental health challenges, you should seek out a mental health provider—or a leader in your faith community if this is part of your life—to help you navigate your way through this significant life transition. You have spent decades of your life working, so of course it will be challenging to adjust to a whole new way of life. Regardless of the specific circumstances of your retirement, preparing for it emotionally and psychologically will help ameliorate the stresses that it can bring so that you can focus on enjoying the life you planned for with a sense of purpose, accomplishment, and connection that lasts.

———————

Ruth C. White is a mental health advocate and stress management expert who often shares her journey of recovery and resilience with bipolar disorder in her talks, workshops, and writings. White has authored four books on mental health, including *The Stress Management Workbook* and *Bipolar 101*. She blogs for *Psychology Today*, writes for *Thrive Global*, and appears frequently as a mental health commentator and educator on KRON4 TV Bay Area. She is the founder of WellMindPlus, a mental wellness consulting firm.

NOTES

1. World Health Organization, "Ageing and Health," Fact Sheet, October 1, 2022, https://www.who.int/news-room/fact-sheets/detail/ageing-and-health.

2. Manuel Pabon-Carrasco et al., "Prevalence of Depression in Retirees: A Meta-Analysis," *Healthcare* 8, no. 3 (2020): 321, https://www.ncbi.nlm.nih.gov/pmc/articles/PMC7551681/.

3. Dhaval Dave, Inas Rashad, and Jasmina Spasojevic, "The Effects of Retirement on Physical and Mental Health Outcomes," Working paper 12123, National Bureau of Economic Research, Cambridge, MA, March 2006, https://www.nber.org/system/files/working_papers/w12123/w12123.pdf.

4. A. Odone et al., "Does Retirement Trigger Depressive Symptoms? A Systematic Review and Meta-Analysis," *Epidemiology and Psychiatric Sciences* 30 (2021): e77, https://www.ncbi.nlm.nih.gov/pmc/articles/PMC8679838/.

5. "Retirement Blues: Taking It Easy Can Be Hard on You," Harvard Health Publishing, July 25, 2018, https://www.health.harvard.edu/mens-health/retirement-stress-taking-it-too-easy-can-be-bad-for-you.

6. Gustavo E. Tafet and Charles B. Nemeroff, "The Links Between Stress and Depression: Psychoneuroendocrinological, Genetic, and Environmental Interactions," *Journal of Neuropsychiatry* 28, no. 2

(2016): 77–88, https://neuro.psychiatryonline.org/doi/10.1176/appi.neuropsych.15030053.

7. Jacob Ausubel, "Older People Are More Likely to Live Alone in the U.S. Than Elsewhere in the World," Pew Research Center, March 10, 2020, https://www.pewresearch.org/fact-tank/2020/03/10/older-people-are-more-likely-to-live-alone-in-the-u-s-than-elsewhere-in-the-world/.

8. "Loneliness and Social Isolation Linked to Serious Health Conditions," Centers for Disease Control and Prevention, April 29, 2021, https://www.cdc.gov/aging/publications/features/lonely-older-adults.html.

9. "Why Saving for Retirement Feels Impossible," CNBC, October 13, 2022, https://www.youtube.com/watch?v=Tk0CWXGpw6o.

10. Nicole Willcoxon, "Older Adults Sacrificing Basic Needs Due to Healthcare Costs," Gallup, June 15, 2022, https://news.gallup.com/poll/393494/older-adults-sacrificing-basic-needs-due-healthcare-costs.aspx.

11. Robert C. Atchley, *The Sociology of Retirement* (Cambridge, MA; New York: Schenkman Pub. Co., 1976).

12. Beth DeCarbo, "Why Hobbies Are So Important in Retirement," *Wall Street Journal,* November 15, 2022, https://www.wsj.com/articles/hobbies-in-retirement-11668191827.

Define Success for Yourself

CHAPTER 19

How Will You Measure Your Life?

by Clayton M. Christensen

Editor's note: Harvard Business School professor Clayton Christensen taught a popular class on
building and sustaining a successful enterprise. He
considered the last session of each term to be his
most important, even though it switched focus from
how to build and sustain a successful enterprise to
how to build and sustain a successful life. Having
watched too many of his own classmates from Harvard Business School end up disappointed with both
their career and their life, he wanted to help his own

Reprinted from *Harvard Business Review*, July–August 2010 (product
#R1007B).

students avoid that fate. He would write three questions on the whiteboard:

1. How can I find happiness in my career?
2. How can I find happiness in my personal life?
3. How can I stay out of jail?

So he focused their attention on the best tools he could offer them to make better decisions in their lives ahead: to create a strategy for your life, to allocate your resources, to consciously build a family culture, and to avoid the "marginal costs" mistake.

At the core, the questions he raised are ones that we should all be asking ourselves at every stage of our career and life. Clay wrote this article for his students, but in the years since its publication, we've heard from readers of all ages from all over the world who have found enormous value in the enduring wisdom of these ideas. I found one idea particularly powerful, the theory of resource allocation, which is how strategy is really formed for businesses. Strategy is not what companies say is most important. Strategy is determined by how companies choose to use their resources day in and day out. The same is true in our personal lives. How we choose to use our personal energy, focus, and time is where we build the real strategy for our lives. For me, personally, that idea was revelatory. After working with Clay on this article, I completely destructed and reconstructed my life so that my resource allocation better matched my personal strategy for my life.

I had a worthy role model in Clay. While he had managed to become one of the world's most respected management thinkers, he was always crystal clear about what mattered most to him. His weekends were devoted to his beloved family and his church, without exception. Clay believed that when we felt fulfilled in our personal lives, we would be more likely to thrive at work. One thing fueled the other.

As you contemplate the road to retirement, I urge you to think about the tools Clay offers in this article. You still have choices to make about how you will spend your own energy, your focus, and your time. Retiring from something is not the same as retiring to something that you will find fulfilling. Are you investing in your personal relationships? Is your life filled with intrinsic motivators? Do you know what you stand for? Does your resource allocation process match that?

I hope you will find this article as powerful as I did—and still do. How will you measure your life? The ideas here can help you answer that question for yourself, whether you're winding down or starting something new.

—Karen Dillon, 2022

Before I published *The Innovator's Dilemma*, I got a call from Andrew Grove, then the chairman of Intel. He had read one of my early papers about disruptive technology, and he asked if I could talk to his direct reports and explain my research and what it implied for Intel. Excited, I flew to Silicon Valley and showed up at the appointed time, only to have Grove say, "Look, stuff has happened. We have only 10 minutes for you. Tell us what your model of disruption means for Intel." I said that I couldn't—that I needed a full 30 minutes to explain the model, because only with it as context would any comments about Intel make sense. Ten minutes into my explanation, Grove interrupted: "Look, I've got your model. Just tell us what it means for Intel."

I insisted that I needed 10 more minutes to describe how the process of disruption had worked its way through a very different industry, steel, so that he and his team could understand how disruption worked. I told the story of how Nucor and other steel minimills had begun by attacking the lowest end of the market—steel reinforcing bars, or rebar—and later moved up toward the high end, undercutting the traditional steel mills.

When I finished the minimill story, Grove said, "OK, I get it. What it means for Intel is . . . ," and then went on to articulate what would become the company's strategy for going to the bottom of the market to launch the Celeron processor.

I've thought about that a million times since. If I had been suckered into telling Andy Grove what he should think about the microprocessor business, I'd have been killed. But instead of telling him what to think, I taught him how to think—and then he reached what I felt was the correct decision on his own.

That experience had a profound influence on me. When people ask what I think they should do, I rarely answer their question directly. Instead, I run the question aloud through one of my models. I'll describe how the process in the model worked its way through an industry quite different from their own. And then, more often than not, they'll say, "OK, I get it." And they'll answer their own question more insightfully than I could have.

My class at HBS is structured to help my students understand what good management theory is and how it is built. To that backbone I attach different models or theories that help students think about the various dimensions of a general manager's job in stimulating innovation and growth. In each session we look at one company through the lenses of those theories—using them to explain how the company got into its situation and to examine what managerial actions will yield the needed results.

On the last day of class, I ask my students to turn those theoretical lenses on themselves, to find cogent answers to three questions: First, how can I be sure that I'll be happy in my career? Second, how can I be sure that my relationships with my spouse and my family become an enduring source of happiness? Third, how can I be sure I'll stay out of jail? Though the last question sounds lighthearted, it's not. Two of the 32 people in my Rhodes scholar class spent time in jail. Jeff Skilling of Enron fame was a classmate of mine at HBS. These were good guys—but something in their lives sent them off in the wrong direction.

As the students discuss the answers to these questions, I open my own life to them as a case study of sorts, to illustrate how they can use the theories from our course to guide their life decisions.

One of the theories that gives great insight on the first question—how to be sure we find happiness in our careers—is from Frederick Herzberg, who asserts that the powerful motivator in our lives isn't money; it's the opportunity to learn, grow in responsibilities, contribute to others, and be recognized for achievements. I tell the students about a vision of sorts I had while I was running the company I founded before becoming an academic. In my mind's eye I saw one of my managers leave for work one morning with a relatively strong level of self-esteem. Then I pictured her driving home to her family 10 hours later, feeling unappreciated, frustrated, underutilized, and demeaned. I imagined how profoundly her lowered self-esteem affected the way she interacted with her children. The vision in my mind then fast-forwarded to another day, when she drove home with greater self-esteem—feeling that she had learned a lot, been recognized for achieving valuable things, and played a significant role in the success of some important initiatives. I then imagined how positively that affected her as a spouse and a parent. My conclusion: Management is the most noble of professions if it's practiced well. No other occupation offers as many ways to help others learn and grow, take responsibility and be recognized for achievement, and contribute to the success of a team. More and more MBA students come to school thinking that a career in business means buying, selling, and investing in companies. That's unfortunate. Doing deals doesn't yield the deep rewards that come from building up people.

I want students to leave my classroom knowing that.

Create a Strategy for Your Life

A theory that is helpful in answering the second question—How can I ensure that my relationship with my family proves to be an enduring source of happiness?—

concerns how strategy is defined and implemented. Its primary insight is that a company's strategy is determined by the types of initiatives that management invests in. If a company's resource allocation process is not managed masterfully, what emerges from it can be very different from what management intended. Because companies' decision-making systems are designed to steer investments to initiatives that offer the most tangible and immediate returns, companies shortchange investments in initiatives that are crucial to their long-term strategies.

Over the years I've watched the fates of my HBS classmates from 1979 unfold; I've seen more and more of them come to reunions unhappy, divorced, and alienated from their children. I can guarantee you that not a single one of them graduated with the deliberate strategy of getting divorced and raising children who would become estranged from them. And yet a shocking number of them implemented that strategy. The reason? They didn't keep the purpose of their lives front and center as they decided how to spend their time, talents, and energy.

It's quite startling that a significant fraction of the 900 students that HBS draws each year from the world's best have given little thought to the purpose of their lives. I tell the students that HBS might be one of their last chances to reflect deeply on that question. If they think that they'll have more time and energy to reflect later, they're nuts, because life only gets more demanding: You take on a mortgage; you're working 70 hours a week; you have a spouse and children.

For me, having a clear purpose in my life has been essential. But it was something I had to think long and hard about before I understood it. When I was a Rhodes scholar, I was in a very demanding academic program, trying to cram an extra year's worth of work into my time at Oxford. I decided to spend an hour every night reading, thinking, and praying about why God put me on this earth. That was a very challenging commitment to keep because every hour I spent doing that, I wasn't studying applied econometrics. I was conflicted about whether I could really afford to take that time away from my studies, but I stuck with it—and ultimately figured out the purpose of my life.

Had I instead spent that hour each day learning the latest techniques for mastering the problems of autocorrelation in regression analysis, I would have badly misspent my life. I apply the tools of econometrics a few times a year, but I apply my knowledge of the purpose of my life every day. It's the single most useful thing I've ever learned. I promise my students that if they take the time to figure out their life purpose, they'll look back on it as the most important thing they discovered at HBS. If they don't figure it out, they will just sail off without a rudder and get buffeted in the very rough seas of life. Clarity about their purpose will trump knowledge of activity-based costing, balanced scorecards, core competence, disruptive innovation, the four Ps, and the five forces.

My purpose grew out of my religious faith, but faith isn't the only thing that gives people direction. For example, one of my former students decided that his purpose was to bring honesty and economic prosperity to his country and to raise children who were as capably committed to this cause, and to each other, as he was. His purpose is focused on family and others—as mine is.

The choice and successful pursuit of a profession is but one tool for achieving your purpose. But without a purpose, life can become hollow.

Allocate Your Resources

Your decisions about allocating your personal time, energy, and talent ultimately shape your life's strategy.

I have a bunch of "businesses" that compete for these resources: I'm trying to have a rewarding relationship with my wife, raise great kids, contribute to my community, succeed in my career, contribute to my church, and so on. And I have exactly the same problem that a corporation does. I have a limited amount of time and energy and talent. How much do I devote to each of these pursuits?

Allocation choices can make your life turn out to be very different from what you intended. Sometimes that's good: Opportunities that you never planned for emerge. But if you misinvest your resources, the outcome can be bad. As I think about my former classmates who inadvertently invested for lives of hollow unhappiness, I can't help believing that their troubles relate right back to a short-term perspective.

When people who have a high need for achievement—and that includes all Harvard Business School graduates—have an extra half hour of time or an extra ounce of energy, they'll unconsciously allocate it to activities that yield the most tangible accomplishments. And our careers provide the most concrete evidence that we're moving forward. You ship a product, finish a design, complete a presentation, close a sale, teach a class, publish a paper, get paid, get promoted. In contrast, investing time and energy in your relationship with your spouse and children typically doesn't offer that same immediate sense of achievement. Kids misbehave every day. It's really not until 20 years down the road that you can put your hands on your hips and say, "I raised a good son or a good daughter." You can neglect your relationship with your spouse, and on a day-to-day basis, it doesn't seem as if things are deteriorating. People who are driven to excel have this unconscious propensity to underinvest in their families and overinvest in their careers—even though intimate and loving relationships with their families are the most powerful and enduring source of happiness.

If you study the root causes of business disasters, over and over you'll find this predisposition toward endeavors that offer immediate gratification. If you look at personal lives through that lens, you'll see the same stunning and sobering pattern: people allocating fewer and fewer resources to the things they would have once said mattered most.

Create a Culture

There's an important model in our class called the Tools of Cooperation, which basically says that being a visionary manager isn't all it's cracked up to be. It's one thing to see into the foggy future with acuity and chart the course corrections that the company must make. But it's quite another to persuade employees who might not see the changes ahead to line up and work cooperatively to take the company in that new direction. Knowing what tools to wield to elicit the needed cooperation is a critical managerial skill.

The theory arrays these tools along two dimensions—the extent to which members of the organization agree on what they want from their participation in the enterprise, and the extent to which they agree on what actions will produce the desired results. When there is little agreement on both axes, you have to use "power tools"—coercion, threats, punishment, and so on—to secure cooperation. Many companies start in this quadrant, which is why the founding executive team must play such an assertive role in defining what must be done and how. If employees' ways of working together to address those tasks succeed over and over, consensus begins to form. MIT's Edgar Schein has described this process as the mechanism by which a culture is built. Ultimately, people don't even think about whether their way of doing things yields success. They embrace priorities and follow procedures by instinct and assumption rather than by explicit decision—which means that they've created a culture. Culture, in compelling but unspoken ways, dictates the proven, acceptable methods by which members of the group address recurrent problems. And culture defines the priority given to different types of problems. It can be a powerful management tool.

In using this model to address the question, How can I be sure that my family becomes an enduring source of happiness?, my students quickly see that the simplest tools that parents can wield to elicit cooperation from children are power tools. But there comes a point during the teen years when power tools no longer work. At that point parents start wishing that they had begun working with their children at a very young age to build a culture at home in which children instinctively behave respectfully toward one another, obey their parents, and choose the right thing to do. Families have cultures, just as companies do. Those cultures can be built consciously or evolve inadvertently.

If you want your kids to have strong self-esteem and confidence that they can solve hard problems, those qualities won't magically materialize in high school. You have to design them into your family's culture—and you have to think about this very early on. Like employees, children build self-esteem by doing things that are hard and learning what works.

Avoid the "Marginal Costs" Mistake

We're taught in finance and economics that in evaluating alternative investments, we should ignore sunk and fixed costs, and instead base decisions on the marginal costs and marginal revenues that each alternative entails. We learn in our course that this doctrine biases companies to leverage what they have put in place to succeed in the past, instead of guiding them to create the capabilities they'll need in the future. If we knew the future would be exactly the same as the past, that approach would be fine. But if the future's different—and it almost always is—then it's the wrong thing to do.

This theory addresses the third question I discuss with my students—how to live a life of integrity (stay out of jail). Unconsciously, we often employ the marginal cost doctrine in our personal lives when we choose between right and wrong. A voice in our head says, "Look, I know that as a general rule, most people shouldn't do this. But in this particular extenuating circumstance, just this once, it's OK." The marginal cost of doing something wrong "just this once" always seems alluringly low. It suckers you in, and you don't ever look at where that path ultimately is headed and at the full costs that the choice entails. Justification for infidelity and dishonesty in all their manifestations lies in the marginal cost economics of "just this once."

I'd like to share a story about how I came to understand the potential damage of "just this once" in my own life. I played on the Oxford University varsity basketball team. We worked our tails off and finished the season undefeated. The guys on the team were the best friends I've ever had in my life. We got to the British equivalent of the NCAA tournament—and made it to the final four. It turned out the championship game was scheduled to be played on a Sunday. I had made a personal commitment to God at age 16 that I would never play ball on Sunday. So I went to the coach and explained my problem. He was incredulous. My teammates were, too, because I was the starting center. Every one of the guys on the team came to me and said, "You've got to play. Can't you break the rule just this one time?"

I'm a deeply religious man, so I went away and prayed about what I should do. I got a very clear feeling that I shouldn't break my commitment—so I didn't play in the championship game.

In many ways that was a small decision—involving one of several thousand Sundays in my life. In theory, surely I could have crossed over the line just that one time and then not done it again. But looking back on it, resisting the temptation whose logic was "In this extenuating circumstance, just this once, it's OK" has proven to be one of the most important decisions of my life. Why? My life has been one unending stream of extenuating circumstances. Had I crossed the line that one time, I would have done it over and over in the years that followed.

The lesson I learned from this is that it's easier to hold to your principles 100% of the time than it is to hold to them 98% of the time. If you give in to "just this once," based on a marginal cost analysis, as some of my former classmates have done, you'll regret where you end up. You've got to define for yourself what you stand for and draw the line in a safe place.

Remember the Importance of Humility

I got this insight when I was asked to teach a class on humility at Harvard College. I asked all the students to describe the most humble person they knew. One characteristic of these humble people stood out: They had a high level of self-esteem. They knew who they were, and they felt good about who they were. We also decided that humility was defined not by self-deprecating behavior or attitudes but by the esteem with which you regard others. Good behavior flows naturally from that kind of humility. For example, you would never steal from someone, because you respect that person too much. You'd never lie to someone, either.

It's crucial to take a sense of humility into the world. By the time you make it to a top graduate school, almost all your learning has come from people who are smarter and more experienced than you: parents, teachers, bosses. But once you've finished at Harvard Business School or any other top academic institution, the vast majority of people you'll interact with on a day-to-day basis may not be smarter than you. And if your attitude is that only smarter people have something to teach you, your learning opportunities will be very limited. But if you have a humble eagerness to learn something from everybody, your learning opportunities will be unlimited. Generally, you can be humble only if you feel really good about yourself—and you want to help those around you feel really good about themselves, too. When we see people acting in an abusive, arrogant, or demeaning manner toward others, their behavior almost always is a symptom of their lack of self-esteem. They need to put someone else down to feel good about themselves.

Choose the Right Yardstick

This past year I was diagnosed with cancer and faced the possibility that my life would end sooner than I'd planned. Thankfully, it now looks as if I'll be spared. But the experience has given me important insight into my life.

I have a pretty clear idea of how my ideas have generated enormous revenue for companies that have used my research; I know I've had a substantial impact. But as I've confronted this disease, it's been interesting to see how unimportant that impact is to me now. I've concluded that the metric by which God will assess my life isn't dollars but the individual people whose lives I've touched.

I think that's the way it will work for us all. Don't worry about the level of individual prominence you have achieved; worry about the individuals you have helped become better people. This is my final recommendation: Think about the metric by which your life will be judged and make a resolution to live every day so that in the end, your life will be judged a success.

Clayton M. Christensen was the Kim B. Clark Professor of Business Administration at Harvard Business School and a frequent contributor to *Harvard Business Review*. **Karen Dillon** is a former editor of *Harvard Business Review*; the coauthor of three books with Clayton Christensen, including the *New York Times* bestseller *How Will You Measure Your Life?*; and the coauthor of *The Microstress Effect* (Harvard Business Review Press, 2023).

Index

Abrahams, Robin, 75
accountability, 97
advance directives, 197
agency, 86
alignment
    of expectations with partners',
        141–142
    person-job, 61
    with purpose, 88–89
Amabile, Teresa M., 21–37,
        175–187
American Express, 140
anchoring bias, 150
anxiety, 42, 183
architects, on boards, 135
Arredondo, Fabiola, 131
Ashkenas, Ron, 94, 95, 96, 97
assumptions, 61
Atchley, Robert, 194
autonomy, 113
availability bias, 150
avocations, 75, 76–77. *See also*
        LABORS acronym

Bailyn, Lotte, 22
Baker, Rob, 59–69
balance, 32–33, 87

The Bankers Investment Trust
        PLC, 128
Basic America Foods, 98
Bataille, Christine D., 11–19
Bath Iron Works, 97–98
beauty, 75, 77–78. *See also*
        LABORS acronym
Bell South, 71
Bezos, Jeff, 152
biases, 148, 150
boardroom capital, 128
boards of directors, 127–136
    cultural intelligence for, 133
    diversity on, 127–128
    financial intelligence for,
        129–130
    intelligence types for, 129–133
    member types on, 135
    relational intelligence for,
        131–132
    retired leaders on, 138
    for retirement, 165–174
    roles on, 132–133, 135
    skill building for, 133–136
    skills for, 128
    strategic intelligence for,
        130–131
Bower, Joseph, 131

Branson, Richard, 152–153
business models, 131

Cairnie, Ruth, 130, 133
Carnegie, Andrew, 18
Carstensen, Laura, 54
certainty, 113
certifications, 121
change
    deciding on drastic, 147–155
    fears around, 42
    how much or how little you
        want, 46
    planning for, 84–85
    routines and, 52
    separation for, 53–54
Chapman, Consuela, 195, 197
Chenault, Ken, 140, 142, 143
Christensen, Clayton M.,
        205–220
Citigroup, 139, 142
Claman, Priscilla, 165–174
Clark, Dorie, 45–47, 119–126
Clasper, Mike, 132–133
coaching, 119–126
Coleman, John, 71–81
commitments
    avoiding premature, 5
    freedom vs., 29, 31
    retiring leaders and, 140–141
communication, 153–154
    relationships and, 183–185
commuting, 29
confirming evidence bias, 150
consolidation phase, 30–31
consulting, 17, 46, 119–126
    marketing for, 124–125
    preparing for, 120
    recruiting clients for, 121,
        124

    skills analysis for, 121
    taking a break before, 125
    teaching vs., 122–123
contract work, 17
control, 114–115
couples
    time together and, 27
Covid-19 pandemic
    lessons from, 51–58, 147–148
    mental health and, 149
Crary, Marcy, 22
creativity, identity bridging and,
        36–37
credibility, 124–125
cultural intelligence, 133, 134
culture creation, 214–216
curriculum vitae, creating,
        123

data junkies, 135
Davis, Scott, 138, 142, 144
decision-making, 147–155
    biases in, 148–149
    communication and, 153–154
    emotional bookends in, 161
    emotions and, 157–162
    identifying the decision for,
        158–159
    identifying your feelings in,
        159–160
    improving input for, 149–151
    improving output in, 151–153
    outsourcing, 150–151
    visualizing success and,
        160–161
demographic shift, 19
Department of Labor, 2
depression, 191
developmental tasks, 26–30
devil's advocates, 150–151

DiBernardo, Albert, 120, 124
diet and nutrition, 26
Dillon, Karen, 94, 95–97, 205–207
disenchantment phase, 197–198
disruptive technology, 207–208
Dutton, Jane, 60

education. *See also* learning
    for consulting, 121
    returning to, 4
Einhorn, Cheryl Strauss, 157–162
emotional bookending, 161, 162
emotional intelligence, 114
emotions, decision-making and, 157–162
Encore.org, 94
English, Tammy, 54
Enron, 209
entrepreneurship, 33–34
envisioning success, 160–161
envisioning the new, 44, 48
Erikson, Erik, 85
exercise, 198
expectations, 141–142, 176–178
    relationships and, 184–185
experience, 108–109
experimentation, 5–6, 28–29
    decision-making and, 152–153
    job crafting and, 67–68
    laying groundwork with, 94–95
    learning from, 55–56
    prototyping with, 48–49
    transitioning and, 96
exploration, 28–29

fairness, 113
Falcon, Silviana, 111–118

family
    culture creation in, 215–216
    identity bridging and, 34–35
    relationship dynamics and, 181–182
    in retirement boards of directors, 167
Feigen, Marc A., 137–144
financial advisers, 167
financial considerations, 21, 45
    for retiring leaders, 138
    stress and, 193–194
financial intelligence, 129–130, 134
flexibility, 16, 31, 107–110
framing bias, 150
Freedman, Marc, 94, 95
freedom, 29, 31
    self-improvement and, 77
    transitioning and, 88–89
"fresh start" effect, 57
friends, 182–183, 197–198
Fripp, Patricia, 46–47
Fromm, Erich, 88–89
future, focusing on, 172–173

geographic considerations, 45–46
    moving and change facilitation, 53–54
    relationships and, 185
Gerontological Society of America, 2
Giesea, Jeff, 41–50
Gillies, Crawford, 129
goals, 103–104, 183
Gratton, Lynda, 3, 11, 16
Grove, Andrew, 207–208
Groysberg, Boris, 75
Guardian Media Group, 131

habit discontinuity, 53–54, 56–57
Haggett, Bill, 97–99
Hall, Douglas T., 22
happiness
    beauty and, 77–78
    creating a strategy for,
        210–213
    defining for yourself, 209–210
    love and, 75, 76
    meaningful work and, 23
    religion and, 79
    service to others and, 80
Haque, Umair, 116–117
Harvard Medical School, 191
*HBR Guide to Crafting Your
    Purpose* (Coleman), 72
health, 21
    advisers, 168
    relationships and, 175–176
    retirement due to, 192
    well-being crafting and,
        63–64
health-care costs, 193
health insurance, 168
Herzberg, Frederick, 209–210
Hesketh, Anthony, 127–136
Hodge, Doug, 139
honeymoon phase, 196–197
humility, 218–219

"I am" statements, 172–173
Ibarra, Herminia, 1–8, 51–58,
    88
identity, 5, 21–37
    activating dormant, 35–36
    grieving for your old, 44
    letting go and, 74
    life restructuring and, 25–30
    meaningful work and, 23

planning for new, 49–50
retiring leaders and, 138–139
work and, 32
identity bridging, 22, 32–35
    defined, 25
insight, 87–88
integrity, 217–218
Intel, 207–208
intelligence types, 129–133
interests and passions, 2, 4. *See
    also* philanthropy
    activating dormant, 35–36
    identity bridging and, 34–35
    purpose and, 75, 76–77
Irving Shipbuilding, 97
isolation, 72, 74, 112, 192–193

Jacobi, Mary Jo, 133
job crafting, 59–69
job loss, 111–118
    open-mindedness and, 115
    retiring vs. finding a new job
        after, 115–117
    self-compassion and, 113
    unmet needs and, 113–114
jobs
    finding consulting, 121–124
    in-between, 115–117
    redesigning, 13, 16–18
    retirement boards of directors
        and, 169–170
Johnson & Johnson, 138, 139
journaling, 114

Kahneman, Daniel, 148
Kameny, Frank, 49–50
Kameny Papers Projects, 49–50
Kindler, Jeff, 143, 144

Knight, Rebecca, 93–99
Kram, Kathy, 22
Kriete, Roxann, 124

labor force participation rates of older workers, 2
LABORS acronym, 75–80
leaders, retirement by, 137–144
learning, 5–6, 209–210
    experimentation and, 55–56
leaves of absence, 17, 125
Lee, Mary Dean, 11–19
legacy, 199
legal advisers, 168
letting go, 74
leveraging expertise, 97–99
Libra Foundation, 98
life restructuring, 22, 25–30
life stages, 3–4
life strategy, 210–213
liminal spaces, 55–56
LinkedIn, 104, 105
living alone, 192–193
lizard brain, 158, 162
location independence, 45–46
longevity, 3–4, 11
    chances of living to 100 and, 16
    financial concerns and, 193–194
    keeping workers engaged and, 12
    planning for change and, 84–85
    purpose and, 73
Los Angeles Clippers, 142
loss, 139
love, 75, 76. See also LABORS acronym

"marginal costs" mistake, 206, 216–218
marketing, 124–125
Massey, Rufus, 71–72, 76
meaning, 23. See also purpose
    happiness and, 95–96
Medicare, 168
mental health, 149, 190–191
mentors and mentoring, 76
    retired leaders in, 142
    retirement boards of directors, 165–174
metaphors, for talking about retirement, 13, 14–16
Michel, Alexandra, 56
Mortensen, Mark, 147–155
motivation, 147, 209–210
    "fresh start" effect and, 57
Mulcahy, Anne, 138–139, 141
Mullen, Sharon, 127–136

"narcissistic and lazy" bias, 54
Naturally Potatoes, 98
networks and networking, 54. See also relationships
    retirement boards of directors and, 165–174
Ng, Gorick, 101–110
Nickisch, Curt, 21–37
Northrop Grumman, 138
not-for-profit work, 143

occupation, 75, 78–79. See also LABORS acronym; work
Oeppen, Jim, 11
The 100-Year Life (Gratton & Scott), 3, 11
open-mindedness, 115

openness, 114–115
O'Rourke, Laing, 128
outsight, 87–88

packing list, creating, 106–107
Paine, Lynn, 131
Parsons, Dick, 139, 141, 142, 143
passions. *See* interests and
    passions
past, future, and present exercise,
    65–67
pension plans, 11–12
permanence, identifying sources
    of, 73–74
personal development, 60, 61
Personalization at Work (Baker),
    60
perspective, 15–16, 115
Pew Research Center, 193
Pfizer, 143
phased approach, 17–18
philanthropy, 13, 18–19
    identity bridging and, 32–35
    retired leaders in, 138,
        143–144
    transitioning with, 31
philosophic tradition, 75, 79–80
pilots, on boards, 135
PIMCO, 139
Pineland Farms, 98
planning, 47, 84–85, 93–99
    deliberately, 104–106
    experts on, 94–97
    figuring out what you want to
        do, 101–110
    four questions to help with,
        45–47
    laying groundwork in, 94–95
    purpose and, 72–75

retirement boards of directors
    for, 165–174
    for retiring leaders, 140
    stress and, 191–192
police, role as on boards, 135
power of attorney documents,
    197
preretirement, 194–195
productivity, 96–97
progress, 23
prototyping, 48–49
purpose, 49–50, 71–81
    avocations and self-improve-
        ment and, 75, 76–77
    beauty and, 77–78
    crafting, 65
    creating a strategy for your life
        and, 210–213
    determining what's important
        and, 95–96
    LABORS acronym and, 75–80
    love and, 75, 76
    occupation and, 75, 78–79
    planning transitions with,
        72–75
    religious or philosophical
        tradition and, 75, 79–80
    separating work from, 116–117
    service to others and, 80
    stress and, 198–199

reconciliation stage, 198–199
reflection, 95, 103–104
reintegration, 56–57
Reinventing You (Clark), 46–47,
    124
relatedness, 113
relational intelligence, 131–132,
    134

relationships, 28–29, 175–187. *See also* spouses/partners
  crafting, 64–65
  creating a strategy for your life and, 210–213
  dynamics of in retirement, 178–183
  finding new, 184
  friends, 182–183
  "narcissistic and lazy" bias and, 54
  philanthropy and, 31
  purpose and, 76
  retirement boards of directors and, 167
  stress and, 192
  talking about retirement and, 183–185
  in transitions, 74–75
relaxation, 29
religion, 75, 79–80, 212–213
religious or philosophical tradition, 75, 79–80. *See also* LABORS acronym
reorientation stage, 198
research, 2–3
resource allocation, 206, 213–214
résumés, 135–136
retirement
  defining for yourself, 14, 15
  designing exciting, 41–50
  early, mortality and, 73
  early, rates of, 2
  factors influencing timing and, 13–14
  job crafting, 59–69
  making the decision on, 26–27
  phased approach to, 17–18
  stages of, 194–199
  talking about, 13, 14–16
  as transition vs. ending, 1–8
retirement day, 195–196
retirement life cycle, 194–199
Rock, David, 113
Rockefeller Foundation, 143
role intelligence, 132–133, 134
role models, 106
routines, 49–50, 198

sabbaticals, 125
Sargent, Leisa, 11–19
Save the Children, 139
SCARF model, 113
Schein, Edgar, 215
school, returning to, 4
Scott, Andrew, 3, 11, 16
self-compassion, 113
self-improvement, 75, 76–77
self-knowledge, 86–87, 141
Sellwood-Taylor, Jo, 127–136
separation, 53–54
service to others, 80. *See also* LABORS acronym
Simon, Herbert, 148
skill crafting, 63
Skilling, Jeff, 209
skills, 4, 106–107
  analyzing for consulting, 121
  for boards, 128, 133–136
  building, 133–136
  retirement boards of directors and, 170–171
social media, 124–125
The Sociology of Retirement (Atchley), 194
Souza, Vanessa, 196–197

spouses/partners
  aligning expectations with, 141–142, 176–178
  involving in the retirement decision, 27
  involving in your reinvention, 48
  relationship dynamics with, 179–181
stability stage, 198–199
stagnation, 75
status, 113
strategic intelligence, 130–131, 134
strategy, 206, 210–213
stress, 189–201
  coping with, 194–199
  financial concerns and, 193–194
  isolation and, 192–193
  mental health and, 190–191
  sources of, 191–194
structure, 25–30, 96–97
  creating stable, 30–31
  for decision-making, 151
  enjoying the lack of, 29–30
  experimenting with, 48
  job loss and, 112
  for retired leaders, 142–143
  routines and, 49–50
  spouses/partners and, 179–181
  stress and, 192
success
  choosing your yardstick for, 219–220
  creating a strategy for your life and, 210–213
  culture creation for, 214–216
  defining, 110, 206–220
  humility and, 218–219

  "marginal costs" mistake and, 216–218
  purpose and, 212–213
  resource allocation for, 213–214
  visualizing, 160–161
succession planning, 120, 137–140
Sugar, Ron, 138, 140, 142, 143–144
syllabi, 123

talking about retirement, 183–185
  metaphors for, 13, 14–16
  naming it, 43
task crafting, 62–63
teaching, 122–123
Thorne, George, 41
Time Warner, 139
timing, 13–14
  of days in retirement, 26, 29
  not rushing, 95
  for retiring leaders, 140–141
  work redesigning and, 13, 16–18
Tools of Cooperation, 214–216
transitioning, 4–5
  allowing time for, 24–25, 43–44
  consolidation phase and, 30–31
  envisioning the new and, 44, 48
  experimentation in, 96
  exploration and experimentation in, 28–29
  getting better at, 83–89
  getting feedback for, 87–88
  identity bridging in, 32–35

leaving gracefully, 85–86
middle period in, 6
pacing and planning, 84–85
paths for, 104–106
planning with purpose, 72–75
retirement boards of directors
    and, 170–171
self-knowledge and, 86–87
struggles in, 31–32
three-part cycle of, 53–57
between times and, 55–56

uncertainty, 48–49
    embracing, 86
    retirement boards of directors
        and, 171–172
The Unspoken Rules (Ng), 102

Valeur, Charlotte, 128
Vaupel, James, 11
volunteering, 31, 198
Vough, Heather C., 11–19

Weldon, Bill, 138, 141, 142, 143
well-being
    crafting, 63–64
    relationships and, 175–176
wheel of life, 44, 48
White, Ruth C., 189–201
Wiens, Kandi, 111–118
Wikipedia, 104, 105
Williams, Ronald A., 137–144
Wittenberg-Cox, Avivah, 83–89
wizard brain, 158, 162
Woertz, Pat, 142
work
    communicating with your cur-
        rent employer and, 153–154

creating new deals in, 13,
    16–18
deciding on drastic changes in,
    147–155
detaching from, 27–28
finding happiness in, 209–210
going off-script for, 13–14
identity based on, 32–33,
    36–37
job crafting and, 59–69
job loss and, 111–118
keeping older workers engaged
    and, 12
leaving gracefully, 85–86
as lifelong journey, 101–110
life structure and, 25–26
meaningful, 23
options for, 3
past, future, and present exer-
    cise for, 65–67
purpose and, 75, 78–79
purpose crafting at, 65
relationship crafting at, 64–65
returners to, 2–3
skill crafting at, 63
task crafting at, 62–63
test-driving possible future,
    46–47
well-being crafting and, 63–64
World Health Organization, 190
Wrzesniewski, Amy, 60

Xerox, 138

"Yes days," 184

Zhang, Richard, 109–110
Zikic, Jelena, 12

Smart advice and inspiration from a source you trust.

If you enjoyed this book and want more comprehensive guidance on essential professional skills, turn to the HBR Guides Boxed Set. Packed with the practical advice you need to succeed, this seven-volume collection provides smart answers to your most pressing work challenges, from writing more effective emails and delivering persuasive presentations to setting priorities and managing up and across.

Harvard Business Review Guides

Available in paperback or ebook format. Plus, find downloadable tools and templates to help you get started.

- Better Business Writing
- Building Your Business Case
- Buying a Small Business
- Coaching Employees
- Delivering Effective Feedback
- Finance Basics for Managers
- Getting the Mentoring You Need
- Getting the Right Work Done

- Leading Teams
- Making Every Meeting Matter
- Managing Stress at Work
- Managing Up and Across
- Negotiating
- Office Politics
- Persuasive Presentations
- Project Management

Notes

Notes

Notes

Notes

Notes

Notes

Notes

Notes

Notes

Notes

Notes